About Island Press

Island Press is the only nonprofit organization in the United States whose principal purpose is the publication of books on environmental issues and natural resource management. We provide solutions-oriented information to professionals, public officials, business and community leaders, and concerned citizens who are shaping responses to environmental problems.

In 2003, Island Press celebrates its nineteenth anniversary as the leading provider of timely and practical books that take a multidisciplinary approach to critical environmental concerns. Our growing list of titles reflects our commitment to bringing the best of an expanding body of literature to the environmental community throughout North America and the world.

Support for Island Press is provided by The Nathan Cummings Foundation, Geraldine R. Dodge Foundation, Doris Duke Charitable Foundation, Educational Foundation of America, The Charles Engelhard Foundation, The Ford Foundation, The George Gund Foundation, The Vira I. Heinz Endowment, The William and Flora Hewlett Foundation, Henry Luce Foundation, The John D. and Catherine T. MacArthur Foundation, The Andrew W. Mellon Foundation, The Moriah Fund, The Curtis and Edith Munson Foundation, National Fish and Wildlife Foundation, The New-Land Foundation, Oak Foundation, The Overbrook Foundation, The David and Lucile Packard Foundation, The Pew Charitable Trusts, The Rockefeller Foundation, The Winslow Foundation, and other generous donors.

The opinions expressed in this book are those of the author(s) and do not necessarily reflect the views of these foundations.

About the Yale School of Forestry and Environmental Studies

Over the century since its founding, the Yale School of Forestry and Environmental Studies has evolved from a professional school of forestry with ten students and two faculty to a unique institution training tomorrow's environmental leaders and managers. Research and teaching efforts have expanded to include not only forestry, but also a wide set of concerns involving the interactions of human societies and natural systems. As Yale's environment school enters its second century, its goals are to become a truly global school of the environment and to provide broad-gauged professional education that equips its graduates to assume influential roles in government, business, nongovernmental organizations, international affairs, journalism, research, and education. Teaching and research are directed at solving local, national, and global problems as well as advancing the science of sustainability.

Worlds Apart

WORLDS

APART

Globalization and the Environment

Edited by

James Gustave Speth

YALE SCHOOL OF FORESTRY
AND ENVIRONMENTAL STUDIES

ISLAND PRESS

Washington • Covelo • London

Library of Congress Cataloging-in-Publication Data.

Worlds apart : globalization and the environment / edited by James Gustave Speth.
    p. cm.
Includes bibliographical references and index.
    ISBN 1-55963-998-9 (acid-free paper) — ISBN 1-55963-999-7 (pbk. :
acid-free paper)
    1. Environmental policy. 2. Globalization—Environmental aspects.
3. Sustainable development. I. Speth, James Gustave.
    GE170.W674 2003
    363.7'05—dc21
                            2003001904

British Cataloguing-in-Publication Data available.

Book design by: Brighid Willson

Printed on recycled, acid-free paper

Manufactured in the United States of America
09 08 07 06 05 04 03 02   8 7 6 5 4 3 2 1

For Catherine, Jim, and Charlie

Contents

Preface

During the Centennial Year of Yale University's School of Forestry and Environmental Studies, the school was host to an impressive group of guest speakers who addressed issues focusing on the relationship between the growing phenomenon of globalization and the quality of the earth's natural environment. In organizing the lecture series, we at the school saw two principal ways in which environmental concerns intersected with globalization.

First, the spread of environmental risks on a global scale and the corresponding migration of environmental policy to the international arena should be seen as important aspects of globalization, broadly defined. Indeed, humanity's first attempt at global environmental governance emerged in the 1980s and 1990s paralleling the rise of international economic management and the World Trade Organization (WTO). Over these two decades, the size of the world economy almost doubled, and both international trade and transnational pollution grew enormously. Inevitably, environmental degradation came to be seen as a global challenge requiring international cooperation on a large scale. We now recognize that our species is a global force with little, if any, competition and that the global-scale problems we face today are more menacing than the predominantly domestic issues that spurred the environmental awakening of the 1960s. For this reason, a governing structure for protecting the natural environment from the powerful externalities of a new, integrated world economic system is essential.

Second, globalization in its narrower economic understanding has significant impacts on the environment and the prospects for sustainability. Many observers believe that these interactions, on balance, are harmful to environmental quality and sustainable development, but this conclusion is not unanimously shared. Some argue that globalization will actually help to solve environmental problems because of a predicted decline in poverty and a general increase in information and knowledge. Whatever its impact, globalization—many claim—is an economic phenomenon that is here to stay, and if we wish to find a pathway to a sustainable future, we must do so within the new context that global markets and economies have established. There are some critics who disagree that globalization is an inevitable force in the future, but even they must respond to the current conditions of the world. In short, globalization represents a collection of economic trends worthy of close scrutiny from an environmental standpoint.

The essays in this volume, most of which grew out of the original lectures at Yale, address these themes. In Chapter 1, I expand upon the two perspectives outlined above: the evolution of global environmental governance and the relationship between the globalization of the economy and the transition to a sustainable society. Chapters 2 through 5 focus chiefly on the first of these themes, the rise of environmental concern on the international level. Jane Lubchenco, in Chapter 2, challenges us with a comprehensive evaluation of the threats to global environmental quality that face humanity. In Chapter 3, Maurice Strong calls upon his extensive experiences over the past three decades and provides the reader with a fascinating outline of the recent history of the international environmental movement. Jose Goldemberg gives a detailed review in Chapter 4 of the problems surrounding energy demand, generation, and consumption and discusses the implications for the earth's natural systems. In Chapter 5, Daniel Esty and Maria Ivanova analyze the state of global environmental governance and propose a structure that they believe would help to address the environmental problems that the international community must work cooperatively to solve.

Chapters 6 through 9 generally discuss the second theme, economic globalization and its impact on environmental quality. Here, the perspectives of our authors differ, sometimes sharply. Robert Kates, in Chapter 6, offers an insightful assessment of globalization and its attendant issues and suggests some ways in which those of us who are interested in protecting the environment can strive to make current economic trends work for our cause. In Chapter 7, Jerry Mander takes a much more critical stance against economic globalization by questioning much of the current economic orthodoxy. He stresses that there are inherent problems in our economic practices that can be solved only by making significant changes in the current system. Wise business choices can make a big difference, claims Stephan Schmidheiny in Chapter 8, and he shares his experience as an international businessman in the field of sustainable forestry. In Chapter 9, Vandana Shiva's critique of globalization picks up where Mander leaves off; drawing on her Indian experience, she stresses the weaknesses and inequities in the current world economic system. And in Chapter 10, I offer an epilogue to the collection: a brief review of the World Summit for

Sustainable Development held in Johannesburg in September 2002 and some personal reflections on environmental governance in the wake of the increasing impacts of globalization.

In reading through these essays, I am reminded that our efforts to build systems that allow us to respond effectively to severe threats of environmental degradation are still in their infancy, but that the challenges we have created for ourselves are far along in their maturation. If we do not act quickly, we likely will lose our opportunity to protect much of what we value in the natural world. I hope that this book will help to move us more swiftly in the direction of solutions that will lead to a true state of sustainability.

I am especially grateful, first of all, to the authors of these chapters who journeyed to Yale, met with students, lectured well, and then worked those lectures into the essays we now have. Kathleen Schomaker was an invaluable associate in our Centennial Lecture Series, and Andrew Ludwig, Timothy Farnham, and Todd Baldwin provided excellent editorial and other support. My deepest appreciation goes to all of them.

—JAMES GUSTAVE SPETH
New Haven, CT

Worlds Apart

CHAPTER 1

Two Perspectives on Globalization and the Environment

James Gustave Speth

To the social scientist, "globalization" refers to the compression of the world and the tightening of all the linkages—economic, political, social, environmental—between developments here and events in far corners of the world. Thomas Friedman says that globalization "shrinks the world from a size medium to a size small." It is a process of integrating not just economies but also cultures, environments, and governments.

Proponents see globalization as helping to cure a multitude of the world's ills. Critics see it as a "false dawn" driven by the "manic logic of global capitalism." But all agree that it is happening, and most believe that it is unstoppable.

Interestingly, a decade before the word globalization became fashionable in the late 1980s, the environmental community both in and out of government was realizing that environmental problems were increasingly transboundary in nature and were reaching global-scale proportions. The early 1980s saw the emergence of an international environmental agenda, and what ensued over the next two decades in response to that agenda can be thought of as the first attempt at global environmental governance. The first part of this chapter discusses environmental globalization, including the emergence of global environmental governance and its effectiveness to date.

Perhaps the only concept as heavy laden with multiple agendas as globalization is "sustainable development." Former President Clinton, a recent convert to sustainable development, has remarked that it is "Aramaic to most people." But within environment and development circles, the words "sustainable development" have become *mots d'ordre* since being popularized by the World Commission on Environment and Development in 1987. The commission offered this now-famous definition: Sustainable

1

development is development that "meets the needs of the present without compromising the ability of future generations to meet their own needs." Most analysts now agree that from an environmental perspective, sustainable development requires living off nature's income rather than consuming natural capital. In the terminology of the economists, it implies non-declining natural assets, at a minimum.

The call for sustainable development was born of conflicting realities. On the one hand, economic expansion will surely occur on a grand scale in the decades ahead. In most countries, rapid economic growth is essential to attack the problem of widespread poverty. On the other hand, environmental quality has been everywhere deteriorating as economic activity has expanded. Conscientious observers have little choice other than to seek a development path that simultaneously sustains environmental resources and alleviates poverty.

Today, the transition to a globalized world is progressing rapidly, but the transition to a sustainable one is not. Some believe that globalization is a prime reason for the failure to realize sustainable development. Others argue that globalization can and should advance the transition to sustainability. The second part of this chapter examines those issues.

Environmental Globalization

The expansion of the human enterprise in the twentieth century, and especially since World War II, was phenomenal. Most familiar is the population explosion. It took all of human history for global population to expand to a billion and a half people by 1900. But over the last century, 1.5 billion people were added, on average, every thirty-three years. Over the last twenty years, global population increased by 50 percent, from 4 billion to 6 billion, with virtually all of the growth occurring in the developing world.

Population may have increased fourfold in the past century, but world economic output increased twentyfold. It took all of history to grow the world economy to $6 trillion by 1950. It now grows by this amount every five to ten years. Since 1960 the size of the world economy has doubled and then doubled again.

Ecologist Jane Lubchenco, in her 1998 address as president of the American Association for the Advancement of Science, noted the significance of these developments:

> The conclusions . . . are inescapable: during the last few decades, humans have emerged as a new force of nature. We are modifying physical, chemical, and biological systems in new ways, at

faster rates, and over larger spatial scales than ever recorded on Earth. Humans have unwittingly embarked upon a grand experiment with our planet. The outcome of this experiment is unknown, but has profound implications for all of life on Earth.

Humanity has entered a new period in its relationship with the natural world. Human influence on the great life-support systems of the planet is pervasive and deep. Human society is now in a radically new ethical position because it is now at the planetary controls. Ecologist Peter Vitousek and his coauthors stated the matter forcefully in a 1997 article in *Science*:

> Humanity's dominance of Earth means that we cannot escape responsibility for managing the planet. Our activities are causing rapid, novel, and substantial changes to Earth's ecosystems. Maintaining populations, species, and ecosystems in the face of those changes, and maintaining the flow of goods and services they provide humanity, will require active management for the foreseeable future.

Scientists are a cautious lot, by and large, so when the most respected issue a plea for "active management of the planet," we must take notice. Indeed, the plea of Vitousek and others is but the latest in a long line of pleas from the scientific community urging that governments and others get serious about the task of protecting the global environment. Starting in the 1980s, governments and others did take notice and began the process of assuming responsibility for planetary management.

What emerged over the past two decades is the international community's first attempt at global environmental governance. The fact that Vitousek and others are still pleading twenty years on suggests that all is not well in this new arena. But it is important to note what has been accomplished to date in the area of global environmental governance:

- An agenda has been defined—an agenda of the principal large-scale environmental concerns of the international community.
- In response to this agenda, a huge upsurge of international conferences, negotiations, action plans, treaties, and other initiatives has occurred. New fields of international environmental law and diplomacy have been born. There are now over 250 international environmental treaties, two-thirds of them signed in recent decades.
- There has been a vast outpouring of impressive and relevant scientific research and policy analysis.
- An ever-stronger international community of environmental and other

nongovernmental organizations (NGOs) has launched increasingly sophisticated campaigns. Initiatives have spanned from global to local, from civil disobedience to restrained think-tank publications.

- National governments as well as multilateral institutions from the United Nations to the international development banks have recognized these concerns and have created major units to address global-scale issues.
- While many multinational corporations are still in denial, many others have moved ahead with impressive steps, often ahead of their governments.
- In the academy, international environmental affairs have become a major subject of academic inquiry and teaching in political science, economics, and other departments. A large body of scholarly analysis now exists.
- The United Nations has sponsored an extraordinary series of milestone events: The 1972 Stockholm Conference on the Human Environment was followed by the 1992 Rio Earth Summit and the 2002 World Summit for Sustainable Development in Johannesburg.

These developments unfolded in the 1980s and 1990s in response to the emergence of an agenda of global-scale environmental concerns. Much as the predominantly domestic environmental agenda of 1970 was forming in the 1960s, the global environmental agenda was quietly taking shape in the 1970s. Throughout the 1970s, a steady stream of publications took a planetary perspective and called attention to global-scale problems. Most were authored by scientists with the goal of taking their findings and those of other scientists to a larger audience. The efforts of Paul Ehrlich, George Woodwell, and John Holdren were notable in this regard. Among the path-breaking publications of the 1970s were the following:

1970 *Man's Impact on the Global Environment,* Report of the Study of Critical Environmental Problems (a scientific group assembled at MIT)

1971 *This Endangered Planet,* Richard Falk

1972 *Exploring New Ethics for Survival,* Garrett Hardin

1972 *The Limits to Growth,* Dennis Meadows et al.

1972 *Only One Earth,* Barbara Ward and Rene Dubos

1978 *The Human Future Revisited,* Harrison Brown

1978 *The Twenty-Ninth Day,* Lester Brown

Also in this period were numerous reports from scientific groups, especially panels and committees organized by the International Council of Scientific Unions, the U.S. National Academy of Sciences, the International Union for the Conservation of Nature (IUCN), and the U.N. Environment Programme (UNEP). These reports included the now-famous 1974 study by Sherwood Rowland and Mario Molina explaining the potential of CFCs to deplete the stratospheric ozone layer. (This remains the only environmental research ever to win the Nobel Prize.) And these reports also included the first effort of the U.S. National Academy of Sciences on the problem of global climate change, the "Charney Report" in 1979, which said most of what one needs to know about climate change to take action. The steady stream of publications from Lester Brown and his team at the Worldwatch Institute added to the effort to lay out the key issues.

Then, around 1980, a second generation of reports appeared that sought to pull the issues together into a coherent agenda for international action. These included the *World Conservation Strategy*, by IUCN and UNEP (1980); "Environmental Research and Management Priorities for the 1980s," by an international group of scientists organized by the Royal Swedish Academy of Sciences (published in *Ambio* in 1983); *The World Environment: 1972–1982*, by a UNEP scientific team (1982); and *The Global 2000 Report to the President* (1980) and its follow-up report, *Global Future: Time to Act*, by U.S. government teams organized by President Carter's Council on Environmental Quality (1981). These syntheses, predominantly scientific efforts, were designed to bring global-scale challenges forcefully to the attention of governments.

Collectively, these reports stressed ten principal concerns:

1. Depletion of the stratospheric ozone layer by CFCs and other gases.
2. Loss of crop and grazing land due to desertification, erosion, conversion of land to nonfarm uses, and other factors.
3. Depletion of the world's tropical forests, leading to loss of forest resources, serious watershed damage (erosion, flooding, and siltation), and other adverse consequences.
4. Mass extinction of species, principally from the global loss of wildlife habitat, and the associated loss of genetic resources.
5. Rapid population growth, burgeoning Third World cities, and ecological refugees.
6. Mismanagement and shortages of freshwater resources.

7. Overfishing, habitat destruction, and pollution in the marine environment.
8. Threats to human health from mismanagement of pesticides and persistent organic pollutants.
9. Climate change due to the increase in "greenhouse gases" in the atmosphere.
10. Acid rain and, more generally, the effects of a complex mix of air pollutants on fisheries, forests, and crops.

Clearly, this new agenda was very different from the mostly domestic one that sparked Earth Day in 1970.

Parallel with these efforts to set an agenda for intergovernmental action were a series of stage-setting developments. Political scientist Keith Caldwell has noted that two developments were needed before the international environmental movement could be born: Environmental policy had to be legitimized at the national level, and the life-sustaining processes of the biosphere had to be perceived as a common concern of all peoples. Caldwell sees the 1972 U.N. Conference on the Human Environment, the Stockholm Conference, ably led by Maurice Strong, as crucial in both respects: It forced many national governments to develop domestic environmental programs—including those in Europe, which were lagging behind the United States at this point—and it legitimized the biosphere as an object of national and international policy and collective management.

The Stockholm Conference also had a further important consequence in the creation of the U.N. Environment Programme (UNEP), which had a major impact in the 1970s in promoting the global agenda. The UNEP made estimates of deforestation and called for international action; it convened the 1977 international conference on desertification; it promoted international agreements on the protection of migratory species; and it promoted the World Climate Program of the International Meteorological Organization, all in the 1970s.

By the mid-1980s, the intellectual and policy leadership of the scientific community, the NGO community (with groups such as IUCN, Worldwatch, and the World Resources Institute), and the UNEP had paid off: A new and international environmental agenda that governments

---

Principal Environmental Treaties

Convention on Trade in Endangered Species, 1973

Convention on the Law of the Sea, 1982
 • Agreement on Straddling and Highly Migratory Fish Stocks, 1995

Vienna Convention for the Protection of the Ozone Layer, 1985
 • Montreal Protocol, 1987

Basel Convention on the Control of Transboundary Movements of Hazardous Wastes and Their Disposal, 1989

Framework Convention on Climate Change, 1992
 • Kyoto Protocol, 1997

Convention on Biological Diversity, 1992
 • Cartagena Biosafety Protocol, 2000

Statement of Principles for a Global Consensus on the Management, Conservation, and Sustainable Development of All Types of Forests, 1992 (The Forests Principles are not a treaty and are not legally binding.)

Convention to Combat Desertification, 1994

Rotterdam Convention on Prior Informed Consent for Certain Hazardous Chemicals and Pesticides, 1998

Stockholm Convention on Persistent Organic Pollutants, 2001

---

would have to address collectively had been established. It would take another decade for governments to respond, but by the mid-1990s most of the ten challenges had become the subject of major international treaties, plans of action, or other initiatives.

In short, the global environmental agenda emerged and moved forward due primarily to a relatively small, international leadership community in science, government, the U.N., and NGOs. These groups took available opportunities to put the issues forward—indeed, they created such opportunities—so that governments had little choice but to take some action. The game that many governments played was to respond but not to respond forcefully.

With this background, it is interesting to compare the emergence of the global agenda of the 1980s with the emergence in the United States of the predominantly domestic agenda a decade earlier. Many of the differences have proven consequential in eliciting corrective action from governments. Consider these contrasts:

- The issues on the U.S. domestic environmental agenda of the 1970s (air and water pollution, hazardous wastes spills, strip-mining, clear-cutting, etc.) tended to be acute, immediate, and understandable by the public. Those on the global agenda tend to be more chronic, more remote (at least in the North), and more technically complicated and thus more difficult to understand and appreciate. Over time these differences have translated into major differences in the degree of public awareness and support.
- The global agenda did not spring bottom-up from actual impacts on people. It was forged top-down at the international level by science, often disputed science; by NGOs, often with circumscribed credibility; and by a tiny U.N. agency—the UNEP—tucked away in Nairobi.
- National laws can be written by a majority of the legislature, but sovereignty requires that in international legislation no government can be compelled to agree or be obligated without its consent. As a result, tough treaties are a rare commodity.
- The domestic environmental agenda in the United States was largely translated into legislation before corporate and other opposition was aroused. Action on the global agenda has been pursued in a context in which corporate and other economic interests are fully alerted and often powerfully opposed.
- The United States, the world's most powerful country, led in the fight for national-level action in the 1970s, but it has largely failed to give international leadership on the global agenda. Indeed, it has frequently been a principal holdout on international environmental agreements.
- The villainy of the global agenda is ambiguous. Global-scale environmental problems cannot be blamed only on big corporations when lifestyles, mismanagement by governments North and South, and other factors are clearly implicated. Increasingly, pollution and other problems come not from something going wrong but from normal life.
- The domestic agenda could be addressed primarily through regulatory means, but the global agenda requires major expenditures by governments, including development assistance to the poorer countries. Unfortunately, development assistance has gone down, not up, since the Earth Summit at Rio.

Given these barriers, it is a wonder that any progress was made on the global agenda. How should we assess the progress of the last two decades during which we have been "on notice" of extraordinary global environmental challenges? A significant list of accomplishments that followed in the wake of the new global agenda's emergence was noted earlier. Also noted were the severe constraints facing those seeking concerted international action. How has the play of these forces worked out over the years?

I can provide only a personal assessment. Looking back, it cannot be said that my generation did nothing in response to the 1980 *Global 2000 Report to the President* and similar alerts. Progress has been made on some fronts, but not nearly enough. There are outstanding success stories, but rarely are they scaled up to the point that they are commensurate with the problem. For the most part, my generation has analyzed, debated, discussed, and negotiated these issues endlessly. We are a generation, I fear, of great talkers, overly fond of conferences. But we have fallen far short on action.

How should we grade the international community's responses to the ten global-scale challenges? The successful effort to protect the ozone layer should secure an Honors, but what of the others? These grades should be low—passes for the international responses on population and acid rain, but failing marks in the other seven areas. It has been ten years since the framework conventions on biodiversity and climate were signed at the Rio Earth Summit, but no meaningful protocols under them protecting climate or saving biodiversity are in effect. The threatening global trends highlighted twenty years ago in the *Global 2000 Report* and elsewhere are still very much with us, ozone depletion being the notable exception.

The results of twenty years of international negotiations are disappointing. It is not that what has been agreed—for example, in the three framework conventions on climate, desertification, and biodiversity—is wrong or useless. These conventions have called attention to the problems and have led to many national plans of action in the three areas. But these agreements do not compel the actions that are needed. The Kyoto Protocol is the first significant step beyond the framework convention in these areas, but it represents only a modest down payment on what is needed and at this writing has not yet entered into force. In general, international environmental law is plagued by vague agreements, imprecise requirements, lax enforcement, and underfunded support. Governments still have a long way to go to make these treaties effective.

The treaties on climate, biodiversity, and other topics establish legal regimes. The principal response of the international community to global-scale environmental challenges to date has been a legal one, often regulatory in nature. Other avenues have been pursued, such as somewhat increased government spending on these issues, but the primary focus has been on developing international environmental law and regulation. This is where most people concerned about these issues, whether in or out of government, have placed their bets; this is where the solutions have principally been sought.

The approach taken to global environmental governance has been excessively legalistic and regime-oriented, has sometimes adopted an old-fashioned command-and-control regulatory approach, and has tended to be one-dimensional, neglecting other useful avenues that might address underlying causes and, indeed, neglecting measures that could help the legal regimes work better.

To be honest, we are at the early stages of the journey to sustainability. Meanwhile, the forward momentum of the drivers of environmental deterioration is great. Former Presidential Science Advisor John Gibbons is fond of saying, "If we don't change direction, we'll end up where we're headed." And today we are moving rapidly to a swift and appalling deterioration of our environmental assets. There is still world enough and time, but the decades immediately ahead are crucial. The next doublings of the world economy cannot resemble those of the past. Governments must bring a new toughness to international environmental law and complement it with serious efforts both to address more directly the underlying drivers of environmental deterioration and to improve dramatically the overall economic and political context that determines whether legal regimes are meaningful or weak and whether they succeed or fail.

Sustainable Development and Economic Globalization: Competing Paradigms?

Has economic globalization been an important driving force in the large-scale environmental deterioration that has occurred in recent decades? A broader question is whether economic globalization has been undermining the prospects for sustainable development. If so, must it continue to do so in the future?

These questions address a reality of immense complexity. They will not yield to simple answers. Arthur Mol, in his *Globalization and Environmental Reform,* sets out to show "that it is not globalization that the [Seattle demonstrators] attack and reject, and that it should not be. Globalization . . . is a multifaceted phenomenon with potentially devastating but also potentially beneficial consequences. The environmental NGOs were particularly afraid—and not without reason—of globalization in its one-sided neo-liberal, economic aspect."

Mol goes on to point out that rigorous analyses of the links between globalization and the environment are scarce. But he notes that those writers who have addressed the subject have typically come to the same conclusions:

> . . . the common view put forward by most scholars was a rather negative one: globalization processes and trends add to environmental deterioration, to diminishing control of environmental problems by modern institutions, and to the unequal distribution of environmental consequences and risks between different groups and societies. The dominance of economic (that is, capitalist) globalization processes is often believed to be the root cause of these detrimental environmental effects. Global political institutions, arrangements, and organizations and a global civil society are believed to be lagging behind.

Martin Khor, director of the Third World Network, is one of the most perceptive critics of current globalization processes. In a recent article, he asks why the implementation of the agreements reached at the Earth Summit, U.N. Conference on Environment and Development (UNCED), in 1992 has "largely failed." His answer is clear:

> The reason for failure is not to be found in the sustainable development paradigm [forged at the UNCED]; rather, the paradigm was not given the chance to be implemented. Instead, intense competition came from a rival—the countervailing paradigm of globalisation, driven by the industrialised North and its corporations, that has swept the world in recent years. This is perhaps the most basic factor causing the failure to realise the UNCED objectives.

Khor characterizes the sustainable development paradigm as incorporating the following: the needs of all countries (big or small); a commitment from the strong to help the weak; a concern with both environment and development; and a realization that the state and the international community must intervene on behalf of the public interest to attain greater social equity and bring about more sustainable patterns of production and consumption.

He sees the globalization paradigm as very different: advocating the reduction or removal of regulations on the market, letting free market forces reign, and granting a high degree of rights and freedoms to the large corporations that dominate the market. Extended to the international level, the globalization paradigm, Khor notes, "advocates liberalisation of international markets, breaking down national economic barriers, and granting rights to corporations to see and invest in any country of their choice without restraints or conditions. Governments should not interfere with the free play of the market, and social or developmental concerns (for instance, obtaining grants from developed countries to aid developing countries) should be downgraded."

Khor believes the main factor in the ascendancy of the market paradigm and the marginalization of the sustainable development paradigm has been "the strong support and aggressive advocacy of the powerful countries" for *both* results. He sees the governments of these countries serving as handmaidens to their private commercial interests, downgrading the United Nations in favor of the Bretton Woods institutions and the WTO, promoting the competitiveness of their economies by minimizing environmental and other standards, and generally giving an increasingly global corporate sector nearly free reign.

Khor is undoubtedly right that the governments of the large-economy (G-7) countries have vigorously pursued the market globalization agenda while badly neglecting the UNCED agenda and its efforts to realize sustainable development. What is more interesting is his assertion that the former has been intentionally at the expense of the latter. My own view is that Khor is basically correct on this point, at least with regard to the United States. Many U.S. policymakers have seen the globalization (market) paradigm as supplanting the need for the sustainable development (partnership) paradigm. "Trade, not aid" has become a Washington mantra. Writing in *The Economist,* the Harvard economist Jeffrey Sachs offered a stinging critique of U.S. policy:

> America has wanted global leadership on the cheap. It was desperate for the developing world and post-communist economies to buy into its vision, in which globalization, private capital flows and Washington advice would overcome the obstacles to shared prosperity, so that pressures on the rich countries to do more for the poorer countries could be contained by the dream of universal economic growth. In this way, the United States would not have to shell out real money to help the peaceful reconstruction of Russia, or to ameliorate the desperate impoverishment and illness in Africa. . . . Washington became skittish at anything or anybody that challenged this vision.

Moreover, even among those U.S. policymakers favorable to environment and development objectives, the priority given to the trade and globalization agenda has tended to occupy the available political space and crowd out sustainable development concerns. Hardly anything is more fatal in Washington, D.C., than having too many top priorities. In the battle for attention, environment and development objectives have typically lost out.

This said, the eclipse of the UNCED commitments has surely been brought about by more than the ascendancy of the globalization paradigm. The post–Cold War period, for example, was supposed to bring a peace dividend of financial and political resources that could have been applied to promoting environmental and development objectives. Instead, the United States and others have been enmeshed in a series of military and peacekeeping engagements, now embracing the war on terrorism, that have consumed much of the available time, energy, and money.

Interestingly, even defenders of globalization do not have much to say for themselves on the environment issue. In their article "The Globalization Backlash," John Mickelthwait and Adrian Wooldridge ask whether globalization is destroying the environment and answer, "not really." They point out that there are other powerful anti-environmental forces at work beyond globalization (they cite $650 billion in annual subsidies for environmentally destructive activities globally) and that multinational corporations are typically better environmental performers than local counterparts. But they concede that, in the short term, increased international trade harms the environment by increasing business activity generally because "business of all sorts tends to despoil the environment." Twice they ask, "How much is greenery worth?"—implicitly acknowledging that there are environmental costs to economic benefits.

There are at least eight reasons to suppose that globalization can exacerbate environmental problems. The critics of economic globalization see in it a set of changes that will make the situation confronting the environment worse. In this critique, economic globalization leads to (1) an expansion of environmentally destructive growth; (2) a decrease in the ability of national governments to regulate and otherwise cope with environmental management challenges; (3) an increase in corporate power and reach; (4) the stimulation of particular sectors such as transportation and energy that have largely negative environmental side effects; (5) the increased likelihood of economic crises; (6) the commodification of resources such as water and the decline of traditional local controls on resource use; (7) the spatial separation of action and impact from responsibility; and (8) the further ascendancy of the growth imperative. All of these claims deserve close scrutiny.

A contrary list of forces can be developed—a set of factors that suggests that globalization may help environmental quality. Global corporations can spread the most advanced environmental management technology and techniques. The strengthening of capacities in government to manage economic affairs can have spillover effects, strengthening environmental management. Globalization can lead to increased incomes, which in turn can lead to governmental revenues for environmental and social programs and to increased public demand for environmental amenity. And increasing international trade in resources such as timber could lead to higher prices, more secure property rights, and larger investments in sustaining forest resources. While something can be said for each of these forces, their effects are certainly farther down the road than most of the negative effects mentioned earlier. Nor, on balance, do they seem as powerful. The result, as the Nobel economist Joseph Stiglitz has noted, is that "globalization today . . . is not working for much of the environment." Nor, in his view, is it "working for many of the world's poor" or "for the stability of the global economy."

Whatever globalization's environmental consequences in the past, the future holds much room for improvement. There are a great many things that can and should be done to green globalization and give it a human face. Indeed, observers have known for many years some of the steps that are required. Over a decade ago, the World Resources Institute convened a distinguished group of thirty Western Hemisphere leaders for a "New World Dialogue on Environment and Development in the Western Hemisphere." Two members of their respective senates, Fernando Henrique Cardoso of Brazil and Al Gore Jr. of the United States would later become the president and the vice president, respectively, of their countries. In its October 1991 Open Letter to the Heads of State and Government of the Americas, this group said the following:

> Realizing this brighter future will require heightened international cooperation, particularly between industrial and developing countries, but also among developing countries. We therefore welcome current initiatives to liberalize trade and to revive growth in our region and more broadly. But these proposals are too limited. They will succeed only in expanding unsustainable and inequitable patterns of growth unless they are complemented by powerful initiatives to promote social equity and to protect the environment. Indeed, there is much reason to believe, based on past experience and current trends, that unless major complementary initiatives are undertaken to bring envi-

ronmental, economic, and social objectives together in the new synthesis called *sustainable development,* liberalizing trade and reviving growth could lead to short-term gains and long-term disaster. More than anything else, the Compact for a New World must be a compact for sustainable development.

The group proposed a North–South compact with eight initiatives, including financial assistance, addressing issues of population, environment, poverty, and development. Liberalization of trade and investment regimes was only *one* of the eight.

Clearly, the push for liberalized trade and investment flows should be complemented by equally concerted efforts on the environmental and social fronts. Needed are adequate development finance as well as norms and rules of the road to guide globalization—to protect and benefit poor countries and poor people, the environment, workers, consumers, and investors. The WTO should be reformed to make it more open and broadly accountable, with different principles and procedures to guide its decisions. On the environment front, there should be a WEO (world environmental organization) to match the WTO, or as Dan Esty and Maria Ivanova advocate in Chapter 5, a global environmental mechanism. More broadly, an international polity should evolve and become as robust as the international economy. Things are badly out of phase. Governance of the international economy, shaky though it is, is far ahead of global governance in other areas. While efforts to promote economic globalization proceed apace through the WTO and elsewhere, policymakers must vigorously pursue reforms and build the institutions needed in the social and environmental areas. As Stiglitz has noted, "The most fundamental change that is required to make globalization work in the way that it should is a change in governance." The policy prescriptions of this new governance are not difficult to discern and, indeed, have been frequently identified.

At the deepest level there is a question well put by J. A. Scholte. "Students of globalization," he notes, "must surely take seriously the possibility that underlying structures of the modern (now globalized) world order—capitalism, the state, industrialism, nationality, rationalism— . . . may be in important respects irreparably destructive." In effect, Scholte is suggesting it is perhaps easy to talk about the greening of economic globalization but tremendously difficult to accomplish.

In the end, the question may be whether societies can free themselves of the enchantment of limitless material expansion and what John Kenneth Galbraith has called the "highly contrived consumption of an infinite variety of goods and services." This question is addressed in a new essay, *Great Transition,* by Paul Raskin and his colleagues in the Global Scenario Group. They believe that many scenarios of world economic, social, and environmental conditions are possible, but they favor a "great transition" based on a "new sustainability paradigm":

> The new paradigm would revise the concept of progress. Much of human history was dominated by the struggle for survival under harsh and meager conditions. Only in the long journey from tool making to modern technology did human want gradually give way to plenty. Progress meant solving the economic problem of scarcity. Now that problem has been—or rather, could be—solved. The precondition for a new paradigm is the historic possibility of a post-scarcity world where all enjoy a decent standard of living. On that foundation, the quest for material things can abate. The vision of a better life can turn to non-material dimensions of fulfillment—the quality of life, the quality of human solidarity and the quality of the earth. . . .
>
> Sustainability is the imperative that pushes the new agenda. Desire for a rich quality of life, strong human ties, and a resonant connection to nature is the lure that pulls it toward the future.

The revolution Raskin and his colleagues see coming a quarter century away is primarily a revolution in social consciousness and values. They envision a time when people attach greatest priority to qualitative fulfillment, social solidarity, and ecological integrity. In 1970, Charles Reich, far ahead of his time, wrote of such a new consciousness in *The Greening of America*: "The new consciousness seeks restoration of the non-material elements of man's existence, the elements like the natural environment and the spiritual that were passed by in the rush of material development." Let us hope that Raskin and his colleagues, in seeing these changes finally occurring thirty years after Reich wrote about them, have given our species enough time to grow up. It is doubtful that the planet can take much more of our heedless childhood.

References

Caldwell, L. 1996. *International Environmental Policy.* Durham, N.C.: Duke University Press.

Esty, D., and M. Ivanova, eds. 2002. *Global Environmental Governance: Options and*

Opportunities. New Haven, Conn.: Yale School of Forestry and Environmental Studies.

French, H. 2000. *Vanishing Borders.* New York: W. W. Norton.

Friedman, T. 1999. *The Lexus and the Olive Tree.* New York: Farrar, Straus, Giroux.

Friedman, T. 2002. "States of Discord—Techno Logic," *Foreign Policy,* March/April, page 64.

Galbraith, J. 1998. "On the Continuing Influence of Affluence," in U.N. Development Programme, *Human Development Report 1998.* Oxford: Oxford University Press, page 42.

Gray, J. 1998. *False Dawn.* London: The New Press.

Greider, W. 1997. *One World, Ready or Not: The Manic Logic of Global Capitalism.* New York: Simon and Schuster.

Kates, R., and W. Clark, chairs. 1999. *Our Common Journey: A Transition Toward Sustainability.* Washington, D.C.: National Academy Press.

Khor, M. 2001. "Globalization and Sustainable Development," *International Review for Environmental Strategies,* Winter, page 209.

Lubchenco, J. 1998. "Entering the Century of the Environment," *Science,* 23 January, page 491.

Mander, J., and E. Goldsmith, eds. 1996. *The Case Against the Global Economy.* San Francisco: Sierra Club Books.

McKibbon, B. 1989. *The End of Nature.* New York: Random House.

McNeill, J. 2000. *Something New Under the Sun: An Environmental History of the Twentieth-Century World.* New York: Norton.

Micklethwait, J., and A. Wooldridge. 2001. "Think Again: The Globalization Backlash," *Foreign Policy,* September/October, page 16.

Mol, A. 2001. *Globalization and Environmental Reform: The Ecological Modernization of the Global Economy.* Cambridge, Mass.: MIT Press, pages 2, 71.

New World Dialogue on Environment and Development in the Western Hemisphere. 1991. *Compact for a New World.* Washington, D.C.: WRI.

Organization for Economic Cooperation and Development. 2001. *OECD Environmental Outlook.* Paris: OECD.

Porter, G., et al. 2000. *Global Environmental Politics.* Boulder, Colo.: Westview Press.

Raskin, P., et al. 2002. *Great Transition.* Stockholm: Stockholm Environment Institute.

Reich, C. 1970. *The Greening of America.* New York: Random House.

Sachs, J. 1998. "Global Capitalism: Making It Work," *The Economist,* September, page 23.

Scholte, J., 1996. "Beyond the Buzzword: Toward a Critical Theory of Globalization," in E. Kofman and G. Youngs, eds., *Globalization.* London: Pinter.

Shabecoff, P. 1996. *A New Name for Peace: International Environmentalism, Sustainable Development, and Democracy.* Hanover, N.H.: University Press of New England.

Speth, J. 1985. "Environment, Economy, Security: The Emerging Agenda," in *Protecting Our Environment: Toward a New Agenda.* Washington, D.C.: Center for National Policy.

Speth, J. 1988. "Environmental Pollution," in *Earth '88: Changing Geographic Perspectives.* Washington, D.C.: National Geographic Society, page 262.

Speth, J., 2002. "A New Green Regime: Attacking the Root Causes of Global Environmental Deterioration," *Environment,* September, page 16.

Speth, J. 2002. "Toward Security for All," *Environmental Law Review,* Vol. 32, page 10480.

Stiglitz, J., 2002. *Globalization and Its Discontents.* New York: W. W. Norton.

Strong, M., 2001. *Where on Earth Are We Going?* Toronto: Texere.

United Nations Development Programme. 1999. *Human Development Report 1999.* New York: Oxford University Press.

U.S. Council on Environmental Quality and Department of State. 1980. *The Global 2000 Report to the President.* Washington, D.C.: U.S. Government Printing Office.

U.S. National Assessment Synthesis Team. 2000. *Climate Change Impacts on the United States.* Cambridge, England: Cambridge University Press.

Vitousek, P., et al. 1997. "Human Domination of Earth's Ecosystems," *Science* 277, page 494.

Woodwell, G. 2001. *Forests in a Full World.* New Haven, Conn.: Yale University Press.

World Commission on Environment and Development. 1987. *Our Common Future.* Oxford: Oxford University Press, page 8.

World Resources Institute. 1991. *Compact for a New World: New World Dialogue on Environment and Development in the Western Hemisphere.* Washington, D.C.: WRI.

World Resources Institute et al. 2000. *World Resources 2000–2001.* Washington, D.C.: WRI, and earlier volumes in this series.

Worldwatch Institute, 2001. *Vital Signs 2001.* New York: W. W. Norton, and other volumes in this series.

Introduction

In this comprehensive chapter, Jane Lubchenco presents the current state of the global environment and what she believes are the elements necessary for making the transition to a more scientifically literate and sustainable society. With a marine biologist's perspective, Lubchenco focuses on the status of the scientific information available to citizens and policymakers and the important role that science must play in informing our environmental decision-making capabilities. She addresses several "myths" related to "assumptions of how the world works," and then concludes with priorities for expanding our knowledge of the natural world and the human impacts upon it.

Lubchenco's discussion of six global-scale indicators of environmental change—based on studies reported in peer-reviewed literature—could serve as a primer for those wishing to understand "some basic messages about current and possible future conditions." From increases in atmospheric carbon dioxide concentrations to human appropriation of more than half of the surface freshwater on the planet, to troubling losses in biodiversity, these are indicators that cannot be ignored, for as Lubchenco declares, they make it evident that the planet's life-support systems are at risk.

Lubchenco's message is ultimately optimistic, as long as science serves as the foundation for the tools that will help the world transition to a sustainable future.

Dr. Jane Lubchenco is the Wayne and Gladys Valley Professor of Marine Biology and Distinguished Professor of Zoology at Oregon State University. She has served as president of both the Ecological Society of America and the American Association for the Advancement of Science, and was named to the National Academy of Sciences in 1996. She was recently elected president of the International Council for Science. She also serves on the boards of numerous environmental groups, including the World Resources Institute and Environmental Defense, as well as on advisory committees for the National Research Council, the National Science Foundation, the United Nations Environment Programme, and UNESCO. Author of many publications, Lubchenco is also the recipient of numerous awards, including a MacArthur Fellowship, a Pew Fellowship, and the 2002 Heinz Award in the Environment.

—J.G.S.

CHAPTER 2

Waves of the Future:
Sea Changes for a Sustainable World

Jane Lubchenco

Waves come in all sizes and energy levels. They can be cataclysmic tsunamis attacking the land, they can combine to create the perfect storm at sea, or—at the opposite end of the spectrum—they can be delightful challenges for surfers during the day or the ideal soporific at night. For most of the history of humans on Earth, the extreme versions of waves and other major forces of nature—floods, volcanoes, earthquakes, and hurricanes—have been among the most serious threats to people and civilizations. Through time, and with ingenuity and humility, humans have learned to cope with these forces of nature. Observation, prediction, and precaution have all played key roles.

Today, as we stand on the verge of a new millennium and ponder the challenges of a new future, we confront a novel force of nature: ourselves. Over time, but most especially over the last century, anthropogenic activities have increasingly altered the chemistry, physical structure, biology, and ecology of our planet in unimaginable ways. Our activities have inadvertently prompted the formation of numerous waves that are already discharging their energy in surprising ways. Moreover, we are in the process of initiating increasingly more waves of various sizes with unpredictable consequences. It is in our interests to understand the endgame of the waves we are generating and to minimize their destructive impact.

We entered this new century with 6 billion people. Current projections for the growth of human population suggest that by the middle of this century there will be close to 9 billion people. Very quickly, our world will have to accommodate 50 percent more people, and that presents a staggering challenge. Meeting even the most basic needs of these additional billions implies greater production and consumption of goods and services, increased demand for land, for energy, and materials, and thus intensified pressure on the environment and on our living resources. These are challenges we have only just begun to understand or acknowledge. We have yet to deal with them in an effective fashion.

There is reason for optimism on many fronts, but we have yet to confront seriously the magnitude of the challenges ahead. The key point is that current patterns of growth, of resource use and generation of wastes are unsustainable. We are already overstressing the life-support systems of the planet in terms of their continued ability to provide the goods and services on which we are ultimately dependent. Moreover, current patterns of use of resources and generation of wastes are exacerbating the existing inequities within and among nations. Our single, biggest challenge, then, is to figure out how to navigate a transition to a sustainable world.

The transition to sustainability has already begun, in part because global population is beginning to stabilize. That is not happening quickly enough, but it is happening. Hastening the transition to a stable population and promoting other dimensions of the needed transition means figuring out how to meet the needs of current and future populations while nurturing and restoring the life-support systems of the planet. It sounds simple, but it is not.

We tend to think of the different challenges we face in a piecemeal fashion. Poverty, disease, climate change, jobs, biodiversity loss, social justice, pollution, education, fisheries collapses, invasive species, national security—these are all viewed as separate issues. Moreover, the socioeconomic issues generally take precedence over the environmental ones. This fragmented approach is myopic and unfortunate, especially because there are subtle but demonstrable connections between and among many of the environmental issues and the socioeconomic ones. Moreover, the fragmentation may inadvertently generate tsunami-like waves.

Fortunately, there is increasing awareness of the importance of many of the large-scale environmental issues. This awareness has not yet reached the point where environment is a true priority in our national politics, but more and more people are paying attention and are concerned. Increasingly, individuals and organizations are coming to understand that environmental topics are in reality moral or ethical issues. So, key elements of making a transition are in the formative stages.

As a scientist, I wish to focus specifically on the ways in which scientific information and understanding can and should inform the transition. One of the key roles of science is to inform our understanding of how our world works and how we depend upon and affect it. I will concentrate on three aspects of this knowledge: (1) factual information about the state of the planet today, (2) a reexamination of some commonly held assumptions about how the world works, and (3) priorities for new knowledge.

Immense Waves of Global Changes Are in Motion

What do we know with certainty about global conditions today? What facts can serve to ground our discussions about the present and future? There is much public confusion about what we know and what we do not know, so let's take stock.

An article in *Science* for which I was an author, "Human Domination of Earth's Ecosystems," was an effort to summarize a series of global-scale indicators of change, based on published documents in the peer-reviewed scientific literature. I will highlight here six global-scale indicators of change that communicate some basic messages about current and possible future conditions.

The first global-scale indicator of change focuses on land transformation. Humans have long been engaged in converting land from one state to another, whether it's cutting down forests to build cities or to graze cattle or flooding floodplains to create water supplies. Over time, the scale of the human enterprise has increased. Today, approximately half of the entire land surface area of the planet has now been transformed by human activities. That is an astounding figure, especially in view of the fact that much of the remaining land area is not very useful to humans.

The second global-scale indicator of change concerns the composition of the atmosphere. Human activities have increased the carbon dioxide concentration of our atmosphere by 30 percent since the beginning of the Industrial Revolution. We also know that human activities are increasing concentrations of other greenhouse gases; and we know that the planet is beginning to warm, most likely as a result of these changes. Even though we do not understand fully the dynamics of the complex climate system, there is strong consensus that human activities are altering Earth's system for regulating climate.

The third global-scale indicator has to do with water, basic to all life. Human activities now utilize more than half of the available surface freshwater on the planet. More than 70 percent of this use goes to agriculture, with the balance used for industrial activities, sanitation, and drinking water. Freshwater shortages and constraints are more severe in some regions than others, but in general, water is going to be a major limiting resource.

The fourth global-scale indicator of change involves one of the principal biogeochemical cycles of the planet, that of nitrogen. There is plenty of nitrogen in the atmosphere, but it is not in a form that is readily usable by most plants. It has to be chemically converted or "fixed," and the principal natural agents of nitrogen fixation are bacteria and algae. Humans contribute additional fixed nitrogen by making fertilizers and burning fossil fuels. Over the last century, these anthropogenic contributions have increased precipitously. Humans have now more than doubled the amount of nitrogen that is being fixed on an annual basis. We are also moving that fixed nitrogen around the planet in new and different ways.

Much of the fertilizer that is intended to help plants grow is not taken up by plants, but is washed away during rainfall events, carried by streams and rivers, and deposited into coastal waters around the world. We are literally changing the chemistry of our oceans, especially coastal waters, because of the massive amounts of nitrogen and other nutrients flowing into them. The increase in the frequency, intensity, and extent of harmful algae blooms—red tides and others—that is happening globally is strongly correlated with this increase in nutrients flowing to coastal waters. Many (though not all) harmful algal populations respond to increases in nutrients by growing explosively.

A second consequence of this nutrient pollution is the appearance of numerous zones of low oxygen (or hypoxia), so-called dead zones, at the mouths of large rivers that drain major agriculture and livestock areas. These hypoxic zones are increasing in size and number globally. The nitrogen and other nutrients stimulate the growth of phytoplankton. When phytoplankton die, they are decomposed by bacteria. The bacteria consume oxygen. Because the phytoplankton are so abundant, oxygen in the water is severely depleted, sometimes below levels where most marine animals can live. Animals that cannot swim out of the hypoxic zone smother. The dead zone that exists in the Gulf of Mexico is the largest one in the Western Hemisphere. It is about the size of Massachusetts and growing. There are now some forty dead zones around the world, all of which have appeared in the last half century. The massive modification of the nitrogen cycle is indeed a huge wave we have inadvertently generated that is wreaking havoc in unintended ways. We can and should decrease the amplitude and destructive power of this wave.

The fifth global-scale indicator of change is the loss of biological diversity. We are entering the sixth mass extinction event of life on Earth, and the first one that has been caused by human activities. Some of the best data we have are for groups of species such as birds and mammals that both fossilize well and are of innate interest to many people. From these records, we know that we have lost more than a quarter of the bird species once on our planet, most of them within the last thousand years and most of them as a direct result of human activities. The best estimates for overall loss of biodiversity suggest that current levels of extinction are likely 100 to 1,000 times greater than "background" levels, that is, the losses that would occur without human activities. On land the losses of biodiversity are driven primarily by habitat destruction and invasive species; in the oceans the losses result from both of those drivers plus overfishing.

The final global-scale indicator of change has to do with fisheries. What fraction of major global fisheries is in trouble or close to it? Forty years ago, 5 percent of the major marine fisheries were fully exploited, overexploited, or depleted. That figure today stands at close to 70 percent. In a very short period of time, we have gone from bountiful seas to seriously depleted oceans. Fishing activities are being shown to result in numerous unintended consequences, including habitat destruction from trawling gear, disruption of marine ecosystems following removal of top predators, endangerment of threatened species due to bycatch, and depletion of reproductive potential triggered by the skewing of sex ratios. Fishery collapses trigger serious social and economic consequences, yet short-term pressures to catch more fish set the stage for future fishery collapses.

Life Support Systems Are at Risk

These six major indicators of change give us an idea of the massive and unprecedented waves of alterations we have inadvertently set in motion. The list does not include everything that's happening, but rather those changes for which we have quantitative information. Their overall message is a compelling one, specifically, that we now live on a human-dominated planet. Humans are now undoubtedly a major global force of nature, whereas before we have only been local forces of nature. We have yet to grasp the full impact of our power or accept the responsibility that comes with it.

Another overarching message from the partial litany of changes is that now is a very different time than ever before. The rates and scales of change brought on by human activities are vastly different than earlier times on Earth. Even some of the kinds of changes are different. For example, we introduce many novel chemical compounds into the environment, some with unforeseen and undesirable consequences. Chlorofluorocarbons (CFCs) that were thought to be totally inert were later discovered to be depleting the ozone layer in the stratosphere. We are now discovering that persistent organic pollutants are also having unintended and potentially very serious consequences. The reality is that we are changing global systems in new ways, at faster rates, and over larger areas than ever before.

Many of the changes human societies are causing result in disruption of the ecosystems on which humans are ultimately dependent. As we destroy habitat, change climate, disrupt the hydrologic cycle, modify biogeochemical cycles, lose species or seriously deplete populations, or fish out the top predators in the oceans, we are disrupting the functioning of a wide variety of ecological systems and impairing the provision of the critical services provided by those systems to humans.

This concept of ecosystem services is essential to understanding the waves we are generating and how they relate to making a transition to sustainability. Many people still think that apart from food and timber, humanity is independent of nature. The reality is that we need not only nature's goods (such as food, fiber, and medicine) but also a wide range of essential services. These services are benefits provided to us as a by-product of the functioning of various ecosystems around the planet. The provision of services is something we take for granted. The regulation of climate, the provision of pollinators, flood control, water purification and filtration, air purification, control of pest outbreaks, carbon sequestration—these are all services that are provided by ecological systems. Protecting these services, and understanding how modified ecological systems can continue to provide these services, is one of the big challenges not only for the scientific community but for humanity as a whole. Ecosystem goods and services are our life-support systems, and they are at risk.

Science Can Help Dampen the Waves

How can we restore and protect the ecosystems that provide such valuable goods and services while at the same time provide at least the basic necessities for our burgeoning population? How can we dampen the waves of change already set in motion and prevent initiating other tsunamis? In other words, how can we make a transition to sustainability? Obviously, this is a multifaceted and serious challenge. One essential element is knowledge. Knowledge alone is insufficient, but it can provide valuable understanding about the world that can inform discussions and action. Some relevant and important scientific knowledge is being shared; some knowledge exists but has not been widely available. In other realms, new knowledge is urgently needed and should be high priority for research. I explore each of these three categories briefly.

Communicating existing scientific knowledge more widely. Multiple vehicles exist for sharing state-of-the-art scientific information with public and policy audiences. Popular books and scientific assessments are increasing in importance.

A number of new books are beginning to share existing scientific knowledge with lay audiences. For example, *Our Common Journey: A Transition Toward Sustainability,* from the National Academy of Sciences, frames the urgency and elements of the challenge confronting society. *Fragile Dominion,* by Simon Levin, provides key insights into the behavior of complex environmental and social systems. *The New Economy of Nature: The Quest to Make Conservation Profitable,* by Gretchen Daily and Kathy Ellison, describes innovative ways of incorporating the latest knowledge about ecosystem services into practical yet visionary decision making at a variety of scales. *A Plague of Rats and Rubbervines: The Growing Threat of Species Invasions,* by Yvonne Baskin, describes new information about the environmental and economic consequences of biological invasions. Each of these books translates complex scientific knowledge in an engaging and accessible manner to the nonspecialist.

A different and complementary vehicle for making the latest scientific knowledge useful and accessible to citizens and policymakers is the scientific assessment—a synthesis of existing knowledge that is relevant to policy decisions, conducted by an independent, credible scientific organization, using peer review. The most useful scientific assessment articulates clearly the levels of certainty the body has in different kinds of information, and projects the likely outcome of different policy options being considered. The Scientific Committee on Problems of the Environment (SCOPE), an interdisciplinary body of the International Council for Science has long provided invaluable international scientific assessments on a number of important topics. New mechanisms for producing international assessments have been created more recently, for example, the Intergovernmental Panel on Climate Change (IPCC), or the Millennium Ecosystem Assessment. Some nations have national bodies such as the U.S. National Research Council that are designed specifically to provide state-of-the-art, credible information to inform decision making. These assessments demonstrate the usefulness of this kind of neutral, synthetic, and peer-reviewed information. Credible, timely, policy-relevant assessments are invaluable tools to assist communities, states, regions, nations, and the international community in formulating sound policy, yet we have too few mechanisms for generating credible assessments for these different spatial scales and the wide range of issues for which assessments would be useful. If governments and citizens wish to have access to scientific assessments, credible institutions must be created or adequately funded to provide them.

Dispelling myths with existing knowledge. Exempting the above treatments, attempts by many scientists to communicate environmental scientific information to lay audiences often miss the mark because scientists are unaware of or do not address some commonly held myths about how the world works. Failure to address these myths directly leads to a disconnect with audiences because the new information being shared has no proper context. The last three decades have produced a wealth of new information about the environment, the sum total of which is often not widely appreciated. For example, the public and policy discourse about various environmental issues often ignores that some environmental changes are irreversible, that average values often do not capture the most important information, that nature is not infinitely resilient, that rates of change are critical, that many environmental changes are highly nonlinear, that some uncertainty in outcomes is inevitable, or that multiple simultaneous changes are likely to produce different results from single-factor changes.

It is a myth, for example, that humans can count on restoring or fixing any serious environmental change. *Jurassic Park* not withstanding, we cannot recreate species once they have gone extinct. The alterations to the climate system already set in motion will likely have very long-lasting and serious consequences. Eliminating invasive species once they are well established is proving to be exceedingly difficult and often impossible. Serial depletion of fishery after fishery appears to have resulted in significant shifts of some ecosystems to a completely different or "alternate stable state" from which recovery is uncertain. Restoring highly degraded coral reefs or wetlands is proving to be much more difficult than anticipated. In each of these cases, our current policies seem to assume that changes are easily reversed, but our track record says otherwise.

It is a myth that many of our environmental challenges are similar to those of the past. I've often heard people say, "Species have always come and gone, so what's different about now?" The reality is that the rate at which species are being lost today is 100 to 1,000 times the typical levels of extinction in the absence of human influence. On other fronts, changes underway are far different from ever before simply because there are so many of them happening simultaneously (e.g., the earlier list of the six global-scale indicators of change), and at increasing rates of change. Never before have so many people altered the planet in such profound ways.

It is also a myth that additional research can eliminate uncertainty.

Uncertainly is inherent in both natural systems and social systems. Although additional research and the attendant knowledge can provide invaluable information, it cannot eliminate uncertainty. Because the earth system is so highly modified by the broad sweep of environmental changes underway, predicting the exact outcome of different policy options is not possible. It is highly useful and instructive to generate likely scenarios that would occur following different policy choices, but there will inevitably be elements of uncertainty in the outcomes. Uncertainty is too often used as an excuse for inaction. A more enlightened attitude would be to select policy options with the least risk of irreversible or serious impairment of life-support systems.

It is a myth that in the course of human civilization, we humans have weaned ourselves from our former dependence on the natural world. The reality is that we depend ultimately on the goods and services provided by the planet's ecosystems. Caring for the environment is a not a luxury, but rather the key to our future. The costs—environmental, human, and economic—of postponing environmental management can be staggeringly high.

These myths permeate many discussions of environmental issues. Part of the challenge in transitioning to a more sustainable world is to address these myths head-on and do a better job of communicating existing knowledge, both the broad scope as well as specific new findings.

A new research agenda to acquire urgently needed information. In parallel to serious efforts to make existing knowledge more widely available and better understood, a significant new effort to acquire urgently needed new information needs to be launched. The seriousness of environmental challenges warrants a significant new investment in environmental, scientific, and engineering research. Three major, lead organizations have recently conducted studies aimed at beginning to define this new research agenda. The National Science Board (the Board of Directors for the U.S. National Science Foundation) in its report *Environmental Science and Engineering for the 21st Century,* and the subsequent NSF framing and planning documents, propose a broad spectrum of new research that could significantly enhance current understanding. The National Academy of Sciences report *Our Common Journey* and follow-up planning documents call for a new commitment to sustainability science and sketches needed directions for research. The International Council for Science in conjunction with other international partners is making significant progress in defining a research agenda and action plan for sustainability science.

Some common themes are emerging from these initial efforts to define a new research agenda. For example, (1) increased interdisciplinary research across the natural, social, economic, behavioral, and engineering sciences will be essential to success; (2) improved understanding of highly nonlinear, complex adaptive systems would greatly facilitate understanding; (3) long-term research and monitoring is essential, but sorely lacking; (4) a research framework that integrates global and local perspectives to shape a "place-based" understanding of the interactions between environment and society is high priority; (5) knowledge and action must be coupled in recognition of the reality that the pathway to sustainability cannot be charted in advance, but will have to be navigated through trial and error and conscious experimentation. These and other themes emphasize the importance of linking environment and development issues more directly, and improving the understanding of the connections between environment and economy, human health, national security, and social justice. These themes present formidable challenges but are nonetheless essential to success. For example, simply asserting that interdisciplinary research is needed is insufficient; explicit mechanisms to promote and sustain interdisciplinary teams must be created.

Citizens and political leaders are and will be asking for more information and for better guidance. The above activities suggest that scientists feel keenly their responsibility to respond. A significant new effort to provide useful and timely information to inform and guide decisions and actions is indeed appropriate.

Hope and Urgency

Despite the immensity of the challenges facing humanity, there are many reasons for hope. Public awareness is increasing, as is active engagement of key groups, including the private sector, the religious community, scientists, women, nongovernmental organizations, and youth. New knowledge, new technologies, new tools, new partnerships are all contributing to the creation of solutions. This momentum is growing and gaining influence. Because human systems are highly nonlinear and can change very rapidly given the right circumstances (witness the collapse of the Soviet Union or the fall of the Berlin Wall), we might see substantial progress under the right circumstances. Change, when it comes, can come rapidly. Our challenge is to help create the knowledge, awareness, tools, and institutions for positive changes to assist in making the transition.

References

Baskin, Y. 2002. *A Plague of Rats and Rubbervines: The Growing Threat of Species Invasions.* Washington, D.C.: Island Press.

Chapin, F., et al. 2000. "Consequences of Changing Biodiversity," *Nature* 405, no. 11, p. 234.

Daily, G.C. and Ellison, K. 2002. *The New Economy of Nature: The Quest to Make Conservation Profitable.* Washington, D.C.: Island Press.

Lubchenco, J. 1998. "Entering the Century of the Environment: A New Social Contract for Science," *Science* 279, p. 491.

Lubchenco, J., et al. 2002. "Lessons from the Land for Protection of the Sea," *Open Spaces* 5(1), p. 10.

National Research Council. 1999. *Our Common Journey: A Transition toward Sustainability.* Washington, D.C.: National Academy Press.

National Science Board. 2000. *Environmental Science and Engineering for the 21st Century.* Washington, D.C.: National Council for Science and the Environment.

Schiermeier, Q. 2002. "How Many More Fish in the Sea?" *Nature* 419(17), p. 662.

Vitousek, P.M., et al. 1986. "Human Appropriation of the Products of Photosynthesis," *Bioscience* 36, no. p. 368.

Vitousek, P.M., et al. 1997. "Human Alteration of the Global Nitrogen Cycle: Causes and Consequences," *Issues in Ecology*, no. 1, p. 4.

Vitousek, P.M., Mooney, H.A., Lubchenco, J., and Melillo, J.M. 1997. "Human Domination of Earth's Ecosystems," *Science* 277, p. 494.

Yoon, C. 1998. "A 'Dead Zone' Grows in the Gulf of Mexico," *The New York Times,* 20 (January), p. F1.

Introduction

In this chapter, Maurice Strong provides us with what might be called a view from one "present at the creation." His rich experience and deep knowledge of the people, initiatives, and organizations that became what is now the professional environmental bureaucracy gives him a remarkable vantage from which to write what amounts to a brief history of the modern international environmental movement. As one who knows the efforts, accomplishments, challenges, and failures of the environmental establishment, he is in a position to look ahead toward what must be achieved in the twenty-first century, the "decisive century for the human species." Strong presents the key issues of "unfinished business" from the 1992 Earth Summit and lays out a road map for what he terms "a new paradigm of cooperative global governance." This paradigm includes a challenging revision of individual and societal behaviors that he believes must be the prime agenda for all mankind if we are to survive in the face of threats to Earth's environment, resource base, and life-support systems—threats that are "far greater . . . than the risks we face or have faced in our conflicts with each other."

Maurice Strong is perhaps best known for the role he played in organizing the Rio Earth Summit, where he served as secretary-general. Twenty years earlier, in 1972, he was the director of the Stockholm Conference on the Human Environment, which arguably elevated environmental issues into the international spotlight for the first time. In the years after Stockholm, Strong became the first director of the U.N. Environment Programme. Currently, he serves as a director of the World Economic Forum Foundation and the chairman of the Stockholm Environment Institute. Strong's combination of business expertise and passion for the environmental security of the global community makes him a truly unique figure in world affairs.

—J.G.S.

CHAPTER 3

Stockholm Plus 30, Rio Plus 10: Creating a New Paradigm of Global Governance

Maurice Strong

The older I get, the more I realize how the course of my life and my interest in the environment and development fields is rooted in my childhood experiences growing up in a small town on the Canadian prairies. I saw what economic breakdown meant to our lives and the lives of those around us. I wondered about the justice and the efficacy of a system that gave rise to such human suffering and why it took the advent of a war to relieve it. I sought solace in nature—in its awesome complexity, its wonders, and its rhythms. I was impressed with the coherence and harmony of nature, which seemed so lacking in the realm of human affairs. These feelings took on more form and substance when in my teens I lived and worked with the Inuit people in the Eastern Arctic. The life and the culture of the Inuit people and their intimate knowledge of and dependence on nature made a profound impression on me. There is nothing like a nighttime that lasts all winter to help develop one's capacity for study, reading, and reflection.

This chapter, however, is not my autobiography. But I want to acknowledge how those early experiences shaped the career decisions that brought me into the development and environment field and helped me to understand the linkages between them. It was this, together with a longtime aspiration to work on the international dimension of these issues in the United Nations, that led me to respond to the invitation of U.N. Secretary-General U Thant in 1970 to come into the United Nations and assume responsibility for organizing the first global intergovernmental conference on the environment, the U.N. Conference on the Human Environment. I accepted with great enthusiasm, particularly as my fascination with the United Nations had been reinforced when I was able to serve briefly in a very junior position there in 1947, only two years after the organization was born.

To understand the significance of that event, and my excitement at playing a role in it, you have to understand the historical background from which the modern environmental movement emerged.

For centuries the dominant attitude toward the natural world was that it existed for the benefit of humankind, to exploit as we saw fit. "The world is made for man, not man for the world," Francis Bacon wrote four hundred years ago. This remained the dominant attitude of people toward nature until recent times, and still today conditions the attitudes of many. But in the nineteenth century, the negative impacts of the industrial revolution and the increased urbanization that arose from it led to the development of a number of voluntary associations that were the precursors of the conservation movement and the broader concepts of environment and sustainable development that evolved from it. England was the home of one of the first of these: the Commons, Open-Spaces, and Footpath Preservation Society established in 1865. In 1888, the Fog and Smoke Committee was created to press for improvement of urban air quality.

In the United States, Henry David Thoreau dramatized the damaging effects on the human spirit and on nature of the encroachment of industrial and urban life into the wilderness areas of New England. George Perkins Marsh of Vermont, in his monumental book *Man and Nature: The Earth as Modified by Human Action,* documented the systematic and pervasive impact of human activity on nature and how it reverberated to undermine human welfare. Theodore Roosevelt was really the first "environmentalist" U.S. president and a champion of what we now call "sustainable development" of natural resources, long before either of these concepts were known.

The insight that humans inflict damage on themselves by damaging nature has become a basic premise of modern environmentalism as it emerged as a major and influential movement during the second half of the twentieth century. Impacts of air and water pollution, urban blight, desecration of natural resources, and undermining of human health and well-being became more widespread and visible. The impacts were dramatically pointed out by Rachel Carson in her influential book *Silent Spring* and the dire projections of the Club of Rome's *Limits to Growth.* In 1970 these works had just begun to foster public awareness and concern in industrialized countries. The decision by the U.N. General Assembly in 1969, on the initiative of Sweden, to hold the U.N. Conference on the Human

Environment had the potential to be a watershed event in the movement for a better environment.

The Stockholm Conference

The conference was held in Stockholm, Sweden, in June 1972—the first of the major global conferences that have done so much to shape the agenda of the United Nations and the world community during the last three decades. It placed the environment issue firmly on the global agenda and provided the political impetus that led to the convening of the several other global conferences on related issues: the Population conferences in Bucharest in 1974 and Cairo in 1994; the Habitat conferences in Vancouver in 1976 and Istanbul in 1996; the Women's conferences in Mexico City in 1975, Copenhagen in 1980, Nairobi in 1985, and Beijing in 1995; and the Social Summit in Copenhagen in 1995. Each of these was patterned on the model pioneered by the Stockholm conference, most notably in providing for substantial participation on the part of civil society organizations.

The environment issue, and the more comprehensive concept of sustainable development that evolved from it, provide a broad framework in which economic, social, population, gender, and human settlement issues could be seen in their systemic relationship to each other and are the common thread that links the agendas and the results of each of these conferences. In this sense, Stockholm was their logical precursor.

Preparations for the Stockholm Conference brought out the deep differences in the perceptions and the interests of developing countries from those of the industrialized countries, which had taken the initiative to have the U.N. General Assembly convene the conference. When I became secretary-general of the conference a year after preparations for it had begun, there was a strong movement on the part of developing countries, led by Brazil, to boycott the Conference. They were deeply suspicious of the motives of the industrialized countries and concerned that their preoccupation with the environmental "fad" would deflect attention and resources from their first priority of dealing with the critical problems of poverty and underdevelopment. They worried, too, that industrialized countries might seek to impose new constraints on developing countries in the name of environment.

The agenda, which the preparatory committee had developed, gave them good reason for these concerns. It was focused primarily on pollution and conservation issues, including the plight of the whales, which were seen as industrialized countries' concerns and did not accord with developing countries' priorities. We had to work hard to revise the agenda to reflect developing-country interests and concerns, including the insistence by developing countries that if they were to cooperate in dealing with global environmental issues, they must receive "new and additional" financial resources from the more industrialized countries that have been largely responsible for creating these problems and have benefited disproportionately from the processes of industrialization and urbanization that gave rise to them.

Lady Jackson, "Barbara Ward," helped us to assemble some of the most brilliant development experts and most vocal critics of the environmental movement—notably, Sri Lanka's Gamani Corea and Pakistan's Mahbub Ul Haq—in an intensive and often heated dialogue on these issues. This culminated in a meeting in a hotel outside of Geneva, Switzerland, that produced the seminal document articulating the essential relationships between environment and development that provided the policy and intellectual underpinnings for the Stockholm Conference. The Founex Report, named after the village in which the meeting was held, argued that while the degradation of the environment in industrialized countries derived largely from production and consumption patterns, the environmental problems in the developing world were largely a result of underdevelopment and poverty. It called for the integration of development and environmental strategies and urged the richer nations in their own interests to provide more funding to help enable the poorer nations to achieve their development goals in an environmentally sound way.

But we still needed a strong political champion of the developing country position to come to Stockholm to promulgate and give effect to developing country views and interests. There was none better suited to this role than Indian Prime Minister Indira Gandhi, who not only committed to attend but allowed me to say this publicly, which enabled developing countries to shift their emphasis from the prospect of boycotting the conference to that of using it as an opportunity to ensure that their interests and concerns were addressed at it. She was clearly the star performer at Stockholm, putting the developing country position succinctly in her memorable statement that "poverty is the greatest polluter."

The Stockholm Conference starkly brought out the differences between the positions of developing and more industrialized countries, but did not resolve them. Indeed, the issues of finance and the basis for sharing responsibilities and costs continue to be the principal source of differences and controversy between developing and more developed countries and have become central to international negotiations on virtually every environment and sustainable development subject, most notably in the climate change and biodiversity conventions. The principal importance of Stockholm was that it established the framework for these negotiations and for the cooperative arrangements they have produced. Most of all, it brought developing countries into a full and influential participation in these processes.

Stockholm led to a proliferation of new environmental initiatives and the creation of the U.N. Environment Programme, headquartered in Nairobi, Kenya, as well as national environmental ministries or agencies in most countries. New nongovernmental organizations sprung up, many of them in developing countries; universities and other professional and policy organizations established their strengths and their environmental programs, as did international organizations and businesses. In addition, important new institutions were established, none that would become more respected or influential than the World Resources Institute, established and built under the leadership of Gus Speth.

The Rio Earth Summit

Despite progress in many areas, however, it became evident by the mid-1980s that, overall, the environment was deteriorating and the population and economic growth largely responsible for this was continuing. In response, the U.N. General Assembly established a World Commission for Environment and Development under the chairmanship of Norway's Gro Harlem Brundtland. Its report, "Our Common Future," made the case for sustainable development as the only viable pathway to a secure and sustainable future for the human community. Its recommendations led to the decision by the U.N. General Assembly in December 1989 to hold the U.N. Conference on Environment and Development. To underscore the importance of this conference, it was decided that it should be held at the summit level, and it is now known universally as the "Earth Summit."

As an event in itself, the U.N. Conference on Environment and Development—the Earth Summit—in Rio de Janeiro in 1992 was clearly remarkable, indeed historic. Never before had so many of the world's political leaders come together in one place, and the fact that they came to consider the urgent question of our planet's future put these issues under an enormous international spotlight. This was helped by the presence at Rio, both in the conference itself and in the accompanying "Global Forum," of an unprecedented number of people and organizations representing every sector of civil society and more than double the number of media representatives than had ever covered a world conference.

The Earth Summit validated the concept of sustainable development that had been articulated by the Brundtland Commission, not as an end in itself, but as the indispensable means of achieving a civilization in the twenty-first century that is sustainable in economic and social as well as environmental terms. The ecological economist Herman Daly summed up well the conditions that would have to be met in this transition to achieve physical sustainability:

• Rates of use of renewable resources must not exceed their rates of regeneration;
• Rates of use of nonrenewable resources must not exceed the rates at which sustainable renewable substitutes are developed;
• Rates of pollution emission must not exceed the assimilative capacities of the environment.

But the Earth Summit also made clear that sustainability can only be achieved through new dimensions of cooperation among the nations and peoples of our planet and, most of all, a new basis for relationships between rich and poor, both within and among nations.

One of the most frustrating aspects of the Earth Summit was the failure to agree on a forestry convention or even on the initiation of a negotiating process that could lead to a convention. Forestry issues, particularly those surrounding the degradation of moist tropical forests, had been an issue that the global environmental community had been concerned with since the mid-1970s. Yet, the struggle to obtain an agreement on the modest set of Forestry Principles underscores the difficulty of obtaining binding commitments from governments on protection of the world's forests, one of its principal and most vulnerable environmental resources. There can be some comfort in the fact that the Convention on Biological Diversity addresses forestry issues. But since Rio, continuing attempts to move the forestry issue forward on the international agenda have not yet produced agreement to begin negotiations on a convention. This is clearly one of the most urgent issues on the international environmental agenda.

Another disappointing aspect of the Rio conference was the weakening of some key issues in Agenda 21—notably, population, energy, and patterns of production and consumption—in order to achieve consensus. Yet, despite these shortcomings, the agreements reached at the Earth Summit represent the most comprehensive program ever agreed upon by governments for the shaping of the human future. The Declaration of Principles agreed upon at Rio reaffirmed and built upon the Stockholm Declaration. Also, the Programme of Action that the conference adopted—Agenda 21—presents a detailed "blueprint" of the measures required to effect the transition to sustainability. The Conventions on Climate Change and Biodiversity, negotiated during preparations for the conference and opened for signature at it, provided the basic legal framework for international agreements on two of the most fundamental global environmental issues. In addition, the conference agreed on initiating a negotiating process that has since produced a Convention on Desertification, an issue of critical importance to a number of developing countries, particularly, the countries of Sub-Saharan Africa, which are among the world's poorest. The fact that these were agreed to by virtually all of the governments of the world, most of them represented at Rio by their head of state, gives them a unique degree of political authority. But, as we have seen since, it does not ensure their implementation.

Beyond Stockholm and Rio

As we now focus on preparations for the thirtieth anniversary of Stockholm and the tenth anniversary of the Earth Summit, which I refer to as 30/10, we must examine the lessons learned in the past three decades. Our focus must be on the future and how we can use this milestone to break the impasse and make the change of course for which Stockholm and Rio prepared the way.

It must be said that overall implementation and follow-up of the Earth Summit agreements has been disappointing. In the more industrialized countries there has been a recession in the political will for environmental action. Developing countries are at the same time experiencing an unprecedented increase in environmental awareness and concern, as their own environmental problems become more visible and acute. But the capacity to deal with these problems is severely constrained by lack of resources and diminishing international assistance. It is an ominous paradox that while evidence of continued environmental deterioration becomes more compelling, the will to deal with them has weakened. As the latest *World Resources* report points out: "Consumption of everything from rice to paper to refrigerators to oil has risen together, all at a cost to the eco-system. The current rate of decline in the long term productive capacity of eco-systems could have devastating implications for humans and the welfare of all species." This is manifest in the accelerating extinction of species, the depletion of fish stocks, the ominous decline of the quality and availability of water for human consumption, and the continued degradation of precious biological resources, to name but a few.

The latest report of the Intergovernmental Panel on Climate Change reinforces the growing evidence that increased greenhouse gas emissions from human sources is accelerating the processes of climate change with ominous implications for the human future. Despite this, on the eve of the Sixth Conference of the Parties to the Climate Change Convention, the prospects for meeting even the modest targets for reducing greenhouse gas emissions set at Kyoto are not promising, and the possibility for setting the more stringent measures that are clearly required are practically nonexistent.

In addition, the funding necessary to move forward with implementation of the conventions on biodiversity and desertification has been disappointing. The Official Development Assistance required to support developing countries in effecting the transition to more sustainable patterns of development and eradicating poverty have continued to decline since Rio.

There are some bright spots. The Global Environment Facility, the only new financial mechanism to emerge from Rio, has been adept and innovative in mobilizing and leveraging its funding of the incremental environmental costs of selective projects. There has been notable progress in the development of new technologies and techniques to abate pollution and reduce the energy and materials content of a unit of production—what the World Business Council for Sustainable Development calls "eco-efficiency." The role of civil society has assumed more and more importance, both in driving the processes of change and in resisting them. The phenomenon commonly referred to as "globalization" has become the focal point for the backlash we are currently witnessing against the very currents of change that have made us the wealthiest civilization ever while deepening the disparities between winners and losers.

For everyone who takes to the streets in Seattle, Washington, Melbourne, and Prague there are many others who quietly share the same concerns and misgivings about globalization. Not that it would be realistic to think that it could—or should—be stopped or rolled back. Rather, the real issues surrounding globalization are how its manifest risks and vulnerabilities, which impact the environment, the social fabric, and the economies of the poor and technologically deprived, can be avoided and how its benefits may be more widely and equitably shared.

Why is this important to those of us who are deeply concerned about the environment and the sustainability of our societies? Because we must see these issues in the broader perspective of cause and effect in which human actions, their impacts immensely increased by technology, are shaping the human future. We have not yet come to terms with the reality that the processes of globalization are systemic in nature, while the mechanisms and institutions through which we manage them are not.

Civil protests against the phantom phenomenon of globalization, and the direct action in Europe targeted at the steep increases in fuel prices, are in my view no mere passing events. Rather, they signal widespread disquiet and diminishing confidence in the ability of our current political and economic governance systems to manage these processes effectively and equitably. It would be unrealistic to think that civil society can somehow replace governments and intergovernmental organizations. Civil society is too diverse, its views too disparate. It lacks, for the most part, the necessary mechanisms of legitimization, accountability, and concerted action. But to underestimate its growing influence would be equally unrealistic.

Communications technology has now given civil society the capacity to organize itself around issues of common concern, whatever may be its differences in other areas. Indeed, at the global level, I believe civil society will function more and more as the "opposition" to the formal systems of governance, but not as an alternative to governments. For the most part, I am confident that it will be a responsible, "loyal" opposition. But this will depend as much on how governments and international organizations respond to the challenges civil society raises, listening to its voices and valuing its views and concerns.

Decisions taken by trade ministers in the World Trade Organization (WTO), by finance ministers in the World Bank, and by central bank governors in the International Monetary Fund (IMF)—to name but a few— may well be within their traditional specialized mandates and expertise. But these decision makers have major impacts on civil society and must be much more open to input from those who have a stake in the decisions.

This does not mean that civil society organizations must be given the same kind of place at the tables of national governments or international organizations, which, for the foreseeable future, will remain the principal elements in the system of governance. It does mean devising new methods of ensuring that the voices of civil society are engaged in the dialogues and negotiations out of which official policies emerge. Fortunately, technology—notably, the Internet—provides the mechanisms for involving millions of people around the world in governing processes. I strongly believe that one of the most urgent priorities of moving toward a more effective system of managing the processes by which we are shaping our future is to establish new mechanisms to enable the views of people to be heard and their concerns and questions to be answered by the officialdom. How much better and more effective this would be than leaving them no alternative but to go to the streets to make their point!

A great deal of this discontent stems from concerns about the unequal distribution of power and wealth between the developed and developing world. But, as their development accelerates, developing countries are contributing more and more to the larger global risks such as those of climate change, ozone depletion, degradation of biological resources, and loss or deterioration of arable lands. China has already become the second largest source of carbon dioxide emissions and will almost certainly succeed the United States to the dubious honor of becoming number one. The prospect of a massive increase in Third World energy consumption over the next thirty years underscores the need for the industrialized world to reduce its environmental impacts in order to leave "space" for developing countries to meet their own needs and aspirations.

China projects that almost 50 percent of its future energy needs will be met by coal and its use of oil and gas will also escalate. This will lead not only to a substantial increase in the importation of fossil fuels, but also to China's "exports" of carbon dioxide emissions. A similar situation exists in varying degrees in other developing countries, notably India. The best investment industrialized countries can make in reducing overall emissions of greenhouse gases is to help developing countries to obtain the latest state-of-the-art technologies and the incremental financing required to enable them to utilize the cleanest possible energy options in meeting their future energy needs. The Clean Development Mechanism to be established under the Kyoto Protocol of the U.N. Framework Convention on Climate Change and the development of commercial trading in emissions credits offer promising prospects of effecting the least cost means of reducing emissions, while providing for new flows of financial resources to developing countries. In addition, I believe it would be both useful and timely for the World Bank and the United Nations to take the lead in establishing a Consultative Group on Clean Energy, based on the successful model of the Consultative Group for International Agricultural Research, to facilitate the process of mobilizing financial and technological resources to give incentives and support to developing countries to opt for clean energy.

The explosion of urban growth in developing countries is giving rise to more and more environmental degradation, and the former antipathy of developing countries toward environmental issues has given way to mounting public awareness and political attention. Indeed, some of the most polluted and unhealthy environments anywhere are in the mega-cities of the developing worlds—for example, Cairo, Manila, Bangkok, Mexico City, and São Paulo. At the same time, accelerating erosion of soils and the cutting down of forests is exacerbating the human and economic consequences of natural disasters, such as the devastating destruction wrought by Hurricane Mitch in Central America and the Yangtze floods in China. This new awareness does not come about because developing countries have started to heed our admonitions that they should not repeat our mistakes, for they are far more influenced by our example than by our exhortations. Rather, it is due to the fact that they are now experiencing so many of the environmental problems that first gave rise to the environmental movement in industrialized countries.

In a recent discussion with China's Premier Zhu Rong Ji in Beijing, I was impressed at his candor in speaking of the lessons that China had learned from recent manifestations of environmental mismanagement, notably, the Yangtze River floods, which exacted such a high cost in both human and economic terms. He said he is committed to doubling the number of trees planted in China in the next ten years and that he personally intends to plant trees when he retires as Prime Minister. Clearly, the developing world, which is destined to cause ever greater environmental impacts, can and must play a crucial role in developing solutions.

The environment issue is the best illustration of the need to bring all key actors into a system of cooperative management and governance, if such a system is to be effective. Certainly, the same is true of other issues that are critical to the common future of humanity. But not all issues need to be dealt with at the global level, and in many cases, the principal global function is to provide the framework, context, and legal regime required to create incentives for actions that can best be taken at the local, national, and regional levels. I am a great believer in the principle of subsidiarity, which calls for all issues to be dealt with at the level closest to the people concerned and at which they can be dealt with most effectively.

Although the complex processes through which human actions are shaping the human future are systemic in nature, the institutions through which we attempt to manage these processes are far from systemic. Governments and industry are organized primarily on a sectoral basis, and academia on the basis of individual disciplines. They are managed primarily through hierarchical structures. Despite a great deal of talk about the need for more systemic, integrated, and multidisciplinary approaches to management and decision making—and some useful but limited progress in this direction—there is still a vast disconnect between our current management and decision-making processes and the real world cause-and-effect system on which it impacts. This dichotomy must be addressed if we are to develop a sustainable system of governance.

The multilateral organizations are clearly not yet prepared for the new generation of tasks that will be required of them. Collectively, these institutions represent an immense reservoir of experience and expertise, which is an invaluable and irreplaceable asset to the world community. Yet paradoxically, although the need for effective multilateral institutions has never been greater, support for them, both political and financial, is less than it has been in any time since their creation. Individually, many of these organizations are weak and in need of reform. But most of all, they need a fundamental restructuring of their mandates and relationships with each other so that they can operate as a system in carrying out the particular functions allocated to them. New arrangements must be put in place to provide for the more effective participation of business and civil society, which are becoming increasingly important actors in respect to many critical issues.

The difficulties of effecting fundamental changes in the current multilateral system are underscored by the experience of Secretary-General Kofi Annan in launching the most extensive and far-reaching program of reform of the United Nations undertaken since its inception. Gus Speth played a leading role in the reform process. Although governments agreed to consider, and almost applauded, the reforms Kofi Annan undertook on his own authority as secretary-general, they have been unwilling to undertake the more radical and fundamental reforms that he recommended, which only governments can do.

For such a global governance system to function effectively, the developing countries must be brought into a full and equitable partnership. We simply cannot secure our own future on our own. In fact, I am convinced that the prospect of a sustainable future for the human community is likely to be decided in the developing countries. What they do will be influenced, perhaps decisively, by what we in the industrialized world do (or fail to do) in forging an equitable, workable, and cooperative set of arrangements with them. Yet, developing countries cannot be denied the right to grow. Neither can they be expected to respond to exhortations to reduce their population growth and adopt stringent environmental controls from those whose patterns of production and consumption have largely given rise to global risks like climate change. This means recognizing the special responsibilities of the traditional industrialized countries to ensure developing countries the access to the capital and technologies they require for their transition to sustainable development and to cooperate fully in measures to protect the planet's future.

A "Change of Course"

While the resource scarcities projected by the Club of Rome's "Limits To Growth" have not materialized, it would be wrong to assume that its basic premise that there *are* limits to growth was wrong. But those limits are likely to be drawn more by the degree to which we can allow human-sourced greenhouse gas emissions to alter the filtering mechanism of the atmosphere, or the amounts of pollutants and toxic substances we can allow to build up in the environment without acceptable levels of damage to human health and life-support systems, than by shortages of raw materials for which technology has provided a wide range of synthetic substitutes. However, human ingenuity and technology are not likely to replace the many species of plant and animal life that are becoming extinct at accelerated rates or the forests and fish stocks that are being depleted through overexploitation. In addition, there are clearly limits to the extent that this environmental degradation can continue without severe risks to human well-being.

While these factors will impose physical and material limits on economic growth, they need not halt the growth process. They simply call for a change in the nature and the content of growth to a mode that is less physical and materials intensive and directed more to serving the cultural, intellectual, and other nonmaterial needs of people. After all, an individual's growth does not end with physical maturity. Beyond this, the nonmaterial dimensions of human growth are the real essence of our lives. Why should this not be so of societies? This dematerialization of growth is to some degree already under way, particularly through the revolution in electronics, which produces products such as CD disks, and the Internet, in which the material content is but a small portion of the total product value. At the same time, technology is making it possible to envisage closed-circuit industrial systems in which waste products are internalized and external environmental impacts kept to acceptable minimum levels.

In their report to the Earth Summit, a distinguished group of world business leaders, led by Swiss industrialist Stephan Schmidheiny [see Chapter 8], made the point that our industrial civilization is not viable and articulated persuasively and that we must make a "change of course" to the development model that is sustainable in environmental and social as well as economic terms. Evidence since then has reinforced the case that to ensure a sustainable future for our civilization we must radically change the existing economic model and literally reinvent our industrial, or more appropriately, postindustrial, civilization. Clearly, we have the knowledge and the technological capacity to do so. What is really lacking is the political will to make fundamental changes in the system and the policies, incentives, penalties, and regulations by which governments motivate the behavior of industry and individuals to provide positive contributions for sustainable development. The Earth Council, an independent group of world leaders and experts formed to monitor progress on Agenda 21, pointed out in a recent report that more than 700 billion dollars is being spent each year on a global basis to subsidize practices that are unsustainable as well as being wasteful of taxpayers' and consumers' money. That money is literally being used to subsidize the destruction of the environment.

While the need for such a change of course has not yet become conventional wisdom, it is increasingly accepted by more and more enlightened business leaders, and in this respect they are ahead of governments. There is already enough evidence to persuade many business leaders that such a change would open up far more opportunities for business than it would foreclose. Governments are not likely to move until the need for a new "eco-economics" becomes more apparent to the public. This change will require more champions, more practical examples, and more public education.

The system of market capitalism, which has become the dominant theology of our times, has demonstrated an unprecedented capacity to generate wealth. But we are now realizing more and more that it also produces a series of deepening imbalances and inequities between the winners and the losers of the great globalization game, with profound implications for the stability and social equilibrium of national societies as well as the world community. It is surely foreseeable that this situation is not sustainable and requires a new generation of economic and social innovation to ensure that our economic and political system can become just as effective at addressing the social and environmental needs of society as it is at producing wealth.

In addition, a demographic dilemma of monumental proportions is in the making. Although there is now evidence that population growth rates in many developing countries are beginning to decline, it is not likely that the world's population will stabilize much before the midpoint of the twenty-first century on a level that is likely to be at least 50 percent higher than the current population. Most of this growth will be concentrated in the developing world, where it will continue to intensify the pressures on scarce land and resources. In the past, these pressures have been relieved by large-scale migration. But today, the borders of the world are closing and new barriers are being erected to the movement of people, particularly the poor and the dispossessed, at the same time as nations compete to provide incentives to attract the privileged minority with the capital and skills that are in short supply.

The more mature industrialized countries are facing the prospect of aging and declining populations. As the pressure of growing populations and poverty, with its attendant conflicts over land and resources, escalates in developing countries, it will inevitably generate strong incentives for the people affected to seek every means, formal and informal, to migrate to the more industrialized countries. Indeed, in my view, this presents one of the most daunting challenges to governance in both industrialized and developing countries in the period ahead and to the prospects for cooperation among them. It is not too much to imagine that it will call into question the basis on which the very sovereignty of nations over their territory and resources is recognized and respected by the international community, particularly when this accords to some nations a disproportionate share of Earth's territory and resources. Thus, the same forces that are driving the need for more cooperation between industrialized and developing countries also contain the seeds of deepening conflict and division that could threaten the prospects of cooperative governance.

A countryman of mine, Professor Thomas Homer-Dixon, cites the growing potential for eco-conflicts as a result of competition for land and other resources that become locally scarce and competition for shared resources like river systems and common areas like the oceans. The difference Canada has had with the United States and its confrontation between Canada and the European Union over diminishing fish stocks are portents of this. In response to this prospect of eco-conflicts, the Earth Council and the World Conservation Union (IUCN), in cooperation with the U.N. University for Peace, are establishing an Ombudsman Centre for Environment and Development to help identify and prevent potential environment- and resource-related conflicts with an international dimension, and to facilitate their peaceful resolution when they occur.

Peace and security are an indispensable precondition to sustainability. Peace with nature and environmental security must be seen as essential components of a sustainable future. Violent conflict and war inflict devastating damage to the environment. Certainly, the human costs such wars and conflicts produce go far beyond the immediate deaths and suffering that result from them by destroying and undermining the resources on which even larger numbers of people depend for their livelihoods. I may add that this essential link between peace and sustainable development is the reason I have recently undertaken to help revitalize the U.N. University for Peace and establish a strategic partnership between it and the Earth Council.

A Change in Values

The sum total of the behavior of individuals is the main source of human impact on the global environment of which the risks of climate change are a principal manifestation. People's behavior is driven ultimately by their own principal values and priorities. The changes called for at the Earth Summit in Rio in 1992 were fundamental in nature and will not come quickly or easily. Individuals often believe that they can make little difference in the larger scheme of things. But they can. Indeed, without individual change there cannot be societal change.

Today, the dominant ethos is that of individual self-interest. I am sure that most people would share my deep belief that individual rights and freedoms constitute the fundamental foundations of our society. But in order to be able to exercise these rights and freedoms, they must be accompanied by acceptance of the disciplines necessary to ensure that all can enjoy them as well as a high sense of responsibility to each other and to future generations. It is this sense of shared responsibility that must be reinforced, for many of the actions that will ensure a secure and sustainable future for those who follow us on this planet require new dimensions of cooperation with others, both at home and internationally.

One of my greatest disappointments in the result of the Earth Summit was our inability to obtain agreement on an Earth Charter to define a set of basic moral and ethical principles for the conduct of people and nations toward each other and the earth as the basis for achieving a sustainable way of life on our planet. Governments were simply not ready for it. But now the Earth Council has joined with many other organizations around the world to undertake this important piece of unfinished business from Rio through a global campaign designed to stimulate dialogue and enlist contributions to the formulation of a People's Earth Charter. This document is intended to be a compelling and authoritative voice of the world's people that will ultimately have a powerful and persuasive influence on governments, hopefully leading to endorsement of an Earth Charter by the United Nations.

The United States plays a central role in both the challenges that I have been citing and the processes by which we must seek to manage them. As the most powerful nation in the world and the primary driver of the forces of globalization that are shaping its future, what the United States does, or fails to do, will be decisive—not only for the future of the world, but for the future of America. However powerful the United States may be, the country simply cannot go it alone in dealing with issues such as climate change, which are global in nature. It is a paradox, and an ominous portent, that the United States, which was the primary creator of today's multilateral system and has been its principal supporter and guardian for most of the post–World War II period, is now increasingly retreating from multilateralism and becoming more and more unilateral in its approach to major international issues.

In the field of development assistance, it was the United States that invented the concept and exhorted others to join in it. Countries have responded, but the United States has retreated to the bottom of the list. To be sure, donors and recipients are tired and frustrated with foreign aid in its traditional form. It is still very much needed by the poorest countries, but for the most part, what developing countries want and need is more fair and equitable access to our markets, to technology, to private investment, and in the treatment of intellectual property. They also seek recognition of the important services they provide to the world community, for example, as the principal custodians of the world's precious biological, wildlife, and genetic resources. Unfortunately, in so many of these areas the United States has moved from being the main leader to the main obstacle.

I want to make clear, however, that I am a great admirer of the United States and am proud of my long and deep links with it. But I believe that the United States is a true leader when it lives up to the best of its own values and traditions, and that its failures and vulnerabilities arise from those occasions on which it is not faithful to them. The world today, in which we are shaping our world of tomorrow, urgently needs the kind of enlightened American leadership that was so largely responsible for the remarkable progress made by the world community since World War II. This leadership does not mean, as some suggest, dilution of U.S. power or subversion of U.S. sovereignty. Rather, it provides a levering of its power in leading and mobilizing the cooperation and resources of others in achieving a more effective exercise of its sovereignty in respect of those issues that it cannot manage alone.

Conclusion

I am persuaded that the twenty-first century will be decisive for the human species. We are now in a very real sense trustees of our own future. The direction of the human future will be largely set in the first decades of this century, for all the evidences of environmental degradation, social tension, and intercommunal conflict have occurred at levels of population and human activity that are a great deal less than they will be in the period ahead. The risks we face in common, from the mounting dangers to the environment, resource base, and life-support systems on which all life on Earth depends, are far greater as we move into the twenty-first century than the risks we face or have faced in our conflicts with each other. A new paradigm of cooperative global governance is the only feasible basis on which we can manage these risks and realize the immense potential for progress and fulfillment for the entire human family, which is within our reach. All people and nations have in the past been willing to accord highest priority to the measures required for their own security. We must give the same kind of priority to civilizational security and sustainability. This will take a major shift in the current political mind-set. Necessity will compel such a shift eventually; the question is, Can we really afford the costs and risks of waiting?

References

Agenda 21. 1992. *Global Partnership for Environment and Development: A Guide to Agenda 21*. Geneva: UNCED.

Carson, Rachel. 1962. *Silent Spring*. Boston: Houghton Mifflin.

Daly, Herman. 1990. "Toward Some Operational Principles of Sustainable Development," *Ecological Economics*, 2 (1990), page 1.

Earth Council. 1996. *Servicing Innovative Financing of Environmentally Sustainable Development*. Washington, D.C.: World Bank.

Intergovernmental Panel on Climate Change. 1990. *Climate Change: The IPCC Scientific Assessment*. Cambridge: Cambridge University Press.

Marsh, George Perkins. 1874. *Man and Nature: The Earth as Modified by Human Action*. New York: Scribner, Armstrong & Co.

Meadows, Donella H., et al. 1974. *The Limits to Growth: A Report for the Club of Rome's Project on the Predicament of Mankind*. New York: Universe Books.

Schmidheiny, Stephan, et al. 1992. *Changing Course: A Global Business Perspective on Development and the Environment*. Cambridge, Mass.: MIT Press.

World Commission on Environment and Development. 1987. *Our Common Future*. Oxford: Oxford University Press.

World Resources Institute. 2000. *World Resources 2000–2001*. Washington, D.C.: World Resources Institute.

Introduction

Jose Goldemberg sees humanity as a force of nature, specifically a "geologic force" that has changed the planet and continues to do so at rates that cannot be sustained. As a physicist and leading expert on global energy, Goldemberg uses energy consumption as both the entry point and the gauge for his discussion of the numerous harmful environmental, economic, and social effects that are concomitants of current energy systems worldwide. He views energy policies as more than just a part of the overall debate about globalization—they may be *the* critical factor for future success or failure. Economic growth, technological modernization, and virtually all types of global development are leading to rapidly increasing energy usage in dangerously unsustainable patterns. Goldemberg presents an example of positive energy development in his native Brazil—the partial replacement of gasoline by ethanol as an automotive fuel—and further points to other areas where energy sustainability may be advanced through international programs and cooperation. Finally, Goldemberg looks at the routes to sustainable energy: greater efficiencies of use, adoption of renewable sources of energy, development of new technologies, and the transfer of these greener systems to the developing world "where most of the growth in energy consumption will take place. . . . " The human population lives on a planet that every day receives "170,000 times more energy than we use." If we cannot learn to better utilize this wealth of power over the next two decades, Goldemberg tells us, our world faces severe problems.

Dr. Jose Goldemberg earned his Ph.D. in Physical Science from the University of São Paulo, where he was rector (president) from 1986 to 1990. He then served the Brazilian government in various capacities: As Secretary of State for Science and Technology, he modernized information systems; as interim Secretary of the Environment, he oversaw Brazil's participation in the Rio Earth Summit; and as Minister of Education, he prepared the proposal to Congress resulting in autonomy for federal universities. He has authored numerous technical papers and books on nuclear physics, environment, and energy, and has served as president of the Brazilian Association for the Advancement of Science. In 2000, Goldemberg was awarded the Volvo Environment Prize for his collaborative work on a new policy-driven approach to the analysis of world energy needs and how those needs could be met in the early decades of this century.

—J.G.S.

CHAPTER 4

Energy and Sustainable Development

Jose Goldemberg

Life on Earth has shown a remarkable resilience to changes in the environment. Humanity, in particular, has adapted well to changing climate since the last glacial age some ten thousand years ago, when much of the Northern Hemisphere was covered by ice and snow. However, all the natural changes in our environment (excluding natural disasters) occurred slowly over extended periods of time—centuries or longer. These changes affected a human population that was quite small in relation to available natural resources, affording a large natural buffer in which humans could adapt.

Since the Industrial Revolution, anthropogenic impacts on the environment have become more extreme. These impacts include air pollution, water pollution, ozone depletion, climate change, depletion of freshwater, soil erosion, coastal and marine degradation, deforestation and loss of biological diversity, toxic chemicals, and hazardous wastes. These environmental stresses are unfolding in short periods of time—decades, not centuries, much less millennia.

Why are these problems important today but not earlier? The answer, according to the great Russian geochemist V. I. Vernadsky, in 1929, is, "Man has become a large-scale geologic force. The chemical face of our planet, the biosphere, is being sharply and consciously changed by man; even greater changes are happening unconsciously." There are 6 billion people on Earth today, and, on average, each consumes 8 tons of mineral resources per year. A century ago, the population was 1.5 billion and consumption was less than 2 tons per capita—the total impact about fifteen times smaller than today. The resources moved around by humans are comparable to the movement of materials by natural forces, such as wind and rain.

Table 4-1. Environmental and Health Problems.

Insult	Human Disruption Index	Share of disruption caused by commercial energy supply (%)	
		Fossil fuel burning	Other
Lead emissions to atmosphere	18.0	41	
Oil added to oceans	10.0		44
Cadmium emissions to atmosphere	5.4	13	
Total sulfur emissions to atmosphere	2.7	85	
Methane flow to atmosphere	2.3		18
Nitrogen fixation (as NO_x and NH_4)	1.5	30	
Mercury emissions to atmosphere	1.4	20	
Nitrous oxide flows to atmosphere	0.5	12	
Particulate emissions to atmosphere	0.12	36	
Non-methane hydrocarbon emissions to atmosphere	0.12		35
Carbon dioxide to atmosphere	0.05	75	

Source: Updated from Holdren, 1992.

Note: The Human Disruption Index is defined as the ratio of human-generated flow to the natural (baseline) flow.

Broadly speaking, environmental problems have many causes, including population growth, the expansion of industry and transportation, intensive agriculture, and even tourism. At the root of many of these problems, however, lies the production and use of energy. (See Table 4-1.) Air pollution, acid rain, and climate change are all primarily caused by burning fossil fuels for electricity and transportation. Nuclear energy is both the leading source of radioactive waste and a paramount source of environmental risk, the latter demonstrated dramatically by Chernobyl. Some deforestation and land degradation are caused by the use of fuelwood for cooking.

Energy is also often important in indirect ways; for example, oil spills degrade and destroy coastal and marine environments. In addition, competition and conflicts over scarce fossil fuel resources are likely to become more common in the future, should fossil fuel use continue to rise.

Currently, only one-quarter of the world population has reached a standard of living that can be considered acceptable. In the low-income economies of the developing world, the gross domestic product (GDP) per capita is only one-tenth as high as in the Organization for Economic

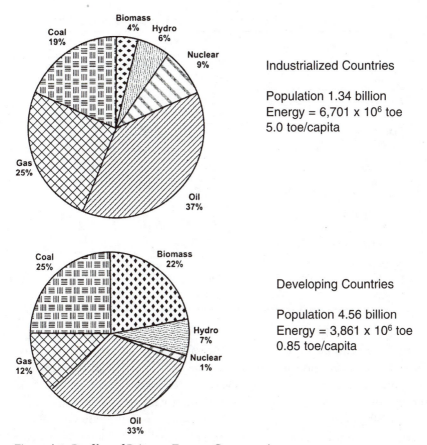

Figure 4-1. Profiles of Primary Energy Consumption.

Cooperation and Development (OECD) countries. Per capita consumption of raw materials and commercial energy is also about ten times smaller (see Figure 4-1).

Per capita energy consumption demonstrates the severity of the discrepancy between rich and poor countries. In 1993, only about 30 percent of all the commercial energy consumption in the world (oil, natural gas, coal, nuclear energy, and hydroelectricity) was used by the 75 percent of people who live in developing countries. The remaining 70 percent of world commercial energy was consumed by the 25 percent of the world population living in industrialized countries.

Worldwide, noncommercial energy accounts for approximately 12 percent of the total fuel mix. But the distribution is uneven: noncommercial

Table 4-2. Total World Primary Energy Consumption (1988).

Source	Primary energy (EJ)	Primary energy (10^9 toe)	% of total
Fossil fuels	320	7.63	78.0
Oil	142	3.39	34.6
Natural gas	85	2.02	20.7
Coal	93	2.22	22.7
Renewables	68	1.62	16.5
Hydro	10	0.23	2.3
Renewable Traditional	50	1.20	12.2
Renewable "New" renewables	8	0.19	2.0
Nuclear	26	0.63	6.3
Nuclear	26	0.63	6.3
TOTAL	414	9.88	100.0

energy represents perhaps 2 percent of total energy consumption in indus-trialized countries compared to an average of 30 percent in the develop-ing world. In some low-income developing countries, traditional biomass energy comprises 90 percent or more of the total energy consumption.

Overall energy consumption in the world and the sources of this energy are given in Table 4-2. The present global growth rate of primary energy use continues to be about 2 percent, which means a doubling of energy consumption by the year 2035, compared to 1998, and a tripling by 2055 (see Table 4-3).

Despite the progress that has been made in many areas around the world in the past few decades, life expectancy is still 30 percent shorter in poor countries than in rich ones; infant mortality is more than three times greater; the fertility rate is five or six children per family as compared to two. Illiteracy in the poorer countries is greater than 40 percent of the population, local pollution is often extreme due to lack of sanitation, and 2 billion people lack access to electricity.

Such disparities will not last forever. Growth and development are fun-damental aspirations of the 75 percent of the world's population who live in the poor countries of Africa, Latin America, the Middle East, and Asia. As a result, the economies of very populous developing countries are

Table 4-3. The Present Energy System. Growth Rate of Primary Energy Consumption.

Global 1970–1998	2.0%/year
Over a 100-year period	2.1%/year
Developing countries (1987–1997)	4.5%/year
Europe (1987–1997)	0.2%/year
U.S.A.–Canada (1987–1997)	1.7%/year
Yearly Global Investments US$ 290–430 billion	

growing rapidly, and in some areas GDP per capita is soon likely to approach the level of developed countries.

As a group, the developing countries' commercial energy use has increased, on average, at a rate three to four times that of the OECD countries—the result of lifestyle changes made possible by rising levels of personal income, coupled with higher population growth rates and a shift from traditional to commercial energy. These trends mean, of course, that more energy resources will be needed to fuel global economic growth and to bring opportunities to billions of people in the developing countries who do not currently have access to adequate energy services.

Conventional wisdom states that economic growth should be roughly proportional to increasing consumption of raw materials and energy. If this relationship were to hold for many more decades, the consequences would be disastrous on environmental, social, and security grounds. Thus, there is a basic potential conflict between environmental well-being and economic development.

More specifically, if industrialized and developing countries continue to rely heavily on fossil fuels as their primary energy supply, regional and global environmental problems such as acid rain and greenhouse warming (caused increasingly by developing countries) will be a serious cause of concern for the industrialized countries and the whole world.

To summarize, the present energy system is not sustainable for the following reasons:

- Modern energy supplies are not accessible to some 2 billion people.
- Wide disparities in access to affordable commercial energy and energy services are inequitable, counter to the concept of human development, and a threat to social stability.

- Unreliable supplies are a hardship and an economic burden for a large portion of the world's population.
- Human health is threatened by high levels of pollution resulting from energy use at household, community, and regional levels.
- The environmental impacts of a host of energy-linked emissions—including suspended fine particles and precursors of acid deposition—contribute to air pollution and degradation of ecosystems.
- Emissions of anthropogenic greenhouse gases, mostly from the energy sector, are altering the atmosphere in ways that may already be having a discernible influence on the global climate system.

After the "oil crisis" of the 1970s, industrialized countries succeeded in reducing their dependence on fossil fuel through improvements in the efficiency of energy use and structural changes in the transition to postindustrial economies. Energy use in the United States, for example, was 35 percent lower in 1990 than it would have been if fossil fuel use had increased in tandem with GDP since 1973. OECD countries also began to shift away from highly polluting, carbon-intensive fuels and started to break the link between economic strength and environmental degradation. Such developments have only begun, but they prove the basic point that economic growth can be significantly decoupled from energy consumption.

There is an indicator that tells us how energy is linked to economic activity in a given country: the energy intensity, which is the ratio of total commercial primary energy supply to the GDP. Usually, noncommercial sources are not included because of the scarcity of reliable data. The evolution of the energy intensity is a useful reference to set up the path of improvements or losses in the efficient use of energy. Moreover, for each country, it can indicate changes in the fuel mix.

Long-term series studies of intensity-of-use curves (measuring mass of material or energy used per unit of income) have shown that, in general, they rise and then fall with further development. Such behavior is particularly striking for curves describing the energy intensity for industrialized countries.

As Figure 4-2 shows, energy intensity grows during the initial phase of industrial development when heavy infrastructure is put in place, peaks, and then declines. Countries that industrialized later go through the same pattern as their predecessors, but with less accentuated peaks. They do not have to reach as high energy intensities because they benefit from modern methods of manufacturing and more efficient systems of transportation. This was true even before the oil crisis of 1973, when rising oil prices

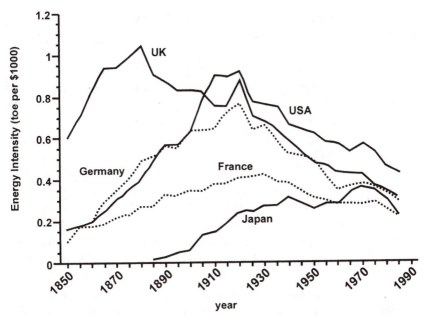

Figure 4-2. Evolution of the Energy Intensity of Industrialized Countries (1850–1990). *Source:* Martin, J.M. (1988), L' Intensité Energetic de L'Activité Economique dans les Pays Industrialisés: les Evolutions de Tres Longes Periode Livrent-elle des Enseignements Utiles? Econimies et Societés—*Cahiers de L'IS-MEA* 22(4): 9–27.

accelerated the pace of energy efficiency improvements in industrialized countries and consequently the reduction in energy intensity. Thus, while the energy intensity of most industrialized countries is decreasing, the energy intensity of most developing countries is increasing (although, in general, it is still lower than industrialized countries).

The strategy of promoting energy efficiency, which was very effective in industrialized countries, is necessary but not sufficient for developing countries. As developing countries build modern economies with the attendant industrial infrastructure, transportation systems, and urban development, growth in commercial energy consumption is inevitable.

Developing countries, however, have a choice: they can mimic the industrialized nations, and go through an economic development phase that is dirty, wasteful, and creates an enormous legacy of environmental pollution; or they can "leapfrog" over some of the steps originally followed by industrialized countries and incorporate modern, efficient technologies into their development process. Least-developed countries (LDCs) are important theaters for innovation and leapfrogging, especially in energy-intensive basic material industries such as steel, chemicals, and cement.

Still, the capacity to choose intelligently among technologies is crucial to the success of leapfrogging. An outstanding example of technological leapfrogging by developing countries, though not in the energy area, is the adoption of cellular telephones to supplement and sometimes replace traditional wired telephone systems. This is happening in certain regions of China and Mongolia. Although cellular telephones were originally developed for mobile uses (or in rural areas where wiring is expensive), technical developments have made them economically competitive for regular service.

The foremost example of technological leapfrogging in developing countries in the energy area is the ethanol program in Brazil. Ethanol is produced from fermented sugarcane juice and used as a substitute for automobile gasoline in Brazil. Approximately 200,000 barrels per day of ethanol are used, reducing by 50 percent the amount of gasoline needed for Brazil's 16.5 million automobiles. Although it has lower caloric content than gasoline, ethanol is an excellent motor fuel: it has a motor octane of 90, exceeding that of gasoline, and is suitable for use in higher compression engines (12:1 versus 8:1).

The expansion of sugarcane plantations from fewer than 1 million hectares in 1975 to 4 million hectares in 1990, and the construction of nearly 400 processing plants to produce large quantities of ethanol, have a resulted in the creation of approximately 700,000 jobs. The initial environmental problems encountered by the distilleries—such as the disposal of liquid effluents and bagasse (dry residues)—have been solved by converting the stillage into fertilizers and using bagasse to generate electricity. In addition, the substitution of ethanol for gasoline avoids emissions of 9.45 metric tons of carbon per year, corresponding to 18 percent of all carbon emissions in Brazil.

In the initial phase of Brazil's ethanol program, the cost of production was very high and ethanol could compete with gasoline only if supported by heavy government subsidies. This is not an unusual situation: the price of any product declines as sales increase, according to "experience" or "learning" curves. Experience curves reflect gains that result from technological progress, economies of scale, and organizational learning. Experience across hundreds of industries shows that the cost of production generally falls exponentially as accumulated productions grows. (See Figure 4-3, which shows the cost evolution of ethanol from 1981 to 1999; ethanol is almost competitive with gasoline at international prices today.)

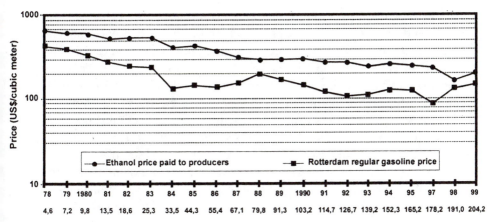

Figure 4-3. Ethanol Costs "Learning Curve." First line indicates year; second line indicates ethanol cumulative production (million cubic meters).

Unlike Brazil, where ethanol is produced from sugarcane, ethanol in the United States is produced from corn, and in Europe from potato or other feedstocks—sources that make a considerable difference from the point of view of sustainability. Almost all the energy needed for the chemical process of preparation of sugarcane juice to ethanol comes from the bagasse, which is energy rich. When the feedstock is corn or potato, the energy needed has to come from fossil fuels. The net energy produced by burning ethanol made from corn or potato can be up to 70 percent less than that required to raise the grain, produce the fuel, and transport it.

Encouraging costly new technologies presents a chicken-and-egg problem. Prices will fall over time, but not without some demand, or at least the anticipation of demand. Yet, if the technology is not competitive at current prices, there may be little "natural" demand. This is why government policies to spur investment and drive demand for selected technologies are so important. Good policy can substantially accelerate the maturation and adoption of good technologies. At the national level, governments can introduce taxes on conventional polluting fuels in order to "level the playing field" to make the new technologies more competitive. Another option is to mandate that the energy portfolio include a fraction of new renewable energy, a policy being pursued by some states. Such "renewable portfolio standards" have now been adopted in seventeen of the United States. At the international level, conventions such as the Climate Convention and the Kyoto Protocol attempt to create such mandates.

Until the 1970s, the prevailing world opinion was that developing countries would have to go through the evolutionary stages characteristic of the industrialized countries, piggybacking on their experiences of centralized, massive-scale, energy-intensive, and highly polluting heavy industries. Conventional wisdom in the rich countries assumed that it would be too risky to finance the introduction in the South of industrial methods not already proven in the North. This begged the question: How can energy supply be approximately tripled to support the future needs of nearly two-thirds of the world's population? Detailed studies recommended coal, gas, and particularly oil, as well as nuclear sources. These sources would create unmanageable air, water, and soil pollution and also aggravate global warming, geopolitical tensions, and nuclear proliferation, which each pose a serious threat to world security. The business-as-usual approach to energy supply for new growth and development in the South appeared to pose an insoluble problem.

My view has been different all along. I believe it might be possible to leapfrog over the experience and know-how of the industrialized countries. The South could develop industries and lifestyles using techniques of efficient energy use, as well as new and renewable energy sources, that had not previously been commercialized in the North. Some of these solutions might even be applicable back in the North.

Southern countries can embark on the use of renewable energy sources in cases where they are well endowed with them; for example, the Philippines and Iceland have abundant geothermal energy, and Brazil has abundant sugarcane plantations. This self-reliant approach reduces the need for fossil fuel imports. Energy conservation, which was adopted in the North after the 1970s energy crisis to reduce oil imports and thus decrease dependence on politically unstable oil exporters, is a strategy of value to both North and South.

We must move in this direction. The important drivers pushing us onto this path to sustainable development are indicated in Table 4-4. A detailed analysis of these drivers and a more sustainable energy future was the object of an important new report—*World Energy Assessment: Energy and the Challenge of Sustainability*—that was released in September 2000. The report was prepared by a group of eminent specialists from different countries and was one of the main inputs to the April 2001 meeting of the Commission of Sustainable Development of the United Nations, which addressed the issue of energy. The report was commissioned by the U.N. Development Programme (UNDP), the Department of Economic and Social Affairs of the United Nations (UNDESA), and the World

Table 4-4. The Drivers to Energy Sustainability.

Problems/Concerns	*Drivers*	*Proposed Solutions*
1. Exhaustion of fossil fuels	Increasing costs Search alternatives Removal of subsidies Inclusion of "externalities" in the cost of energy.	Energy efficiency
2a. Local and regional environmental quality	Desire to improve quality of air and water	Cleaner fossil fuels, filters, catalysts
2b. Global warming	Need to avoid climate change Switch to renewables; CO_2 recapture	Reduced use of fossil fuels
3. Security of supply	Need to guarantee low prices and abundant supply International energy flows Switch to renewables	Greater reliance on indige- nous energy resources
4. Safety	Avoidance of major disasters, particularly nuclear Safe storage of spent nuclear fuel	Intrinsically safe reactors
5. Equity	Avoidance of social unrest and humanitarian concerns "Leapfrogging"	Policies that stimulate supplying energy services to the poor

Energy Council (WEC), which represents energy industries in almost a hundred countries worldwide.

The *World Energy Assessment* (WEA) is neither a manifesto nor a "new" Club of Rome document. It is in part an analysis of what will happen under a business-as-usual scenario with respect to energy resources, given that more than 80 percent of energy used today comes from fossil fuels (coal, oil, and gas). The WEA also explores the likely consequences of adopting new policies and measures to meet the challenges synthesized in the report. Most important, the WEA makes clear that there are technical solutions to all the problems that make the current energy system unsustainable:

- Improve the efficiency of energy use, which could prolong the life of existing reserves and reduce environmental concerns. Many cost-effective steps have already been taken (although much remains to be done) in this direction since the "oil crisis" of the 1970s, but these have not been sufficient to reduce the rate of growth of energy consumption.

- Increase the contribution of renewable energy sources such as wind and photovoltaics, and, most importantly, modernize the use of biomass. Biomass is widely used in developing countries in very inefficient ways. "Modern" renewable sources represent only 2 percent of the world's consumption today but are growing at 30 percent per year.

- Accelerate the development of new technologies such as fuel cells, adopt methods of using coal in cleaner ways than currently practiced (including carbon sequestration), and expand the utilization of hydrogen. Increased financial flows to research and development might be needed to meet these objectives. Several international institutions, such as the GEF (Global Environment Facility), UNDP, and World Bank, as well as some governments (e.g., Germany and the Netherlands) have extensive programs working in these areas. Some of these technologies might not be competitive today, but as they are introduced in the market, their cost will be driven down, as is usually the case with new technologies.

The WEA also tries to forecast which energy scenarios might have the strongest attributes of sustainable development. In Figure 4-4, "traditional" biomass (the dominant form of energy until the middle of the nineteenth

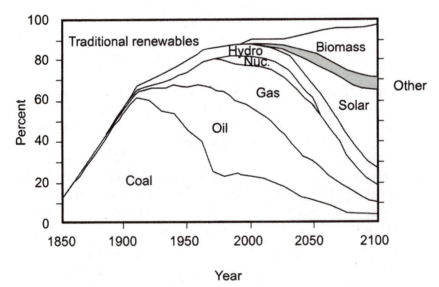

Figure 4-4. Profile of Primary Energy Consumption: Ecologically Driven Scenario.

century) will come back as "modern" biomass—that is, transformed in liquids or gases—while other solar energy technologies (such as wind and photovoltaics) will replace coal, oil, gas, and possibly nuclear energy.

The WEA points out that market forces alone, as they now operate, will not steer the global energy system to a more sustainable direction, despite the inherently dynamic and creative ways the private sector works. Public policies, such as the removal of subsidies to conventional energy and the inclusion of some environmental costs in the price of energy, are needed to facilitate a change. Market forces, with their great dynamism, are clearly the best method of introducing this change, but only if properly guided by regulations. International collaboration could also lead to the transfer of modern and "clean" technologies to the developing countries, where most of the growth in energy consumption will take place in the next few decades. Such transfer would accelerate the leapfrogging process outlined earlier.

Conclusion

The adoption of technologies that could lead to a sustainable energy future must begin now and continue to fruition over the next twenty years. New technologies are, in general, developed in the North where there is a long tradition of innovation and private and governmental support for research and development. Technology is transferred to the South in the form of products in which the technology is built—such as in automobiles or pharmaceuticals. The cost of development of the product is usually recovered by the inventor/industrialist charging a small percentage or royalty on each unit sold. Traditional market mechanisms will lead to the adoption of sustainable energy technologies, but they can be accelerated by government intervention and/or bilateral or multilateral agreements between countries in the North and South.

Our present energy use patterns will not carry us into the future. We must employ innovation—both technological and political—in finding ways to use our resources in the most efficient and environmentally friendly ways possible. The sun bombards the earth every day with 170,000 times more energy than we use. If harnessed properly and distributed equitably, energy will not be an impediment to the sustainable development of humankind.

Reference

Goldemberg, Jose, ed. 2000. *World Energy Assessment: Energy and the Challenge of Sustainability.* New York: UNDP.

Introduction

In this chapter about the creation, design, and deployment of a global environmental mechanism (GEM), Daniel Esty and Maria Ivanova set themselves a daunting but necessary task: describing an animal that does not yet exist, but which—they believe—must be brought into being soon if current cycles of global environmental decline are to be arrested and reversed. Esty and Ivanova discuss threats that can be combated only by a worldwide governance mechanism more effective than the current mix of overlapping, fragmented, contradictory, and often competing bodies. Having made the case that today's markets, environmental issues, and populations are globally interdependent, Esty and Ivanova identify what is not working in the current (dis)order of environmentally concerned systems and agencies, and then sketch out the specifics of a GEM: what it would consist of, how it would work, what it would do differently, and how it could benefit the global environment. Their concise argument will make the reader wonder how, without an "extraordinary mix of political idealism and pragmatism," we would be able to create a "sleeker . . . more efficient architecture that will better serve environmental, governmental, public, and business needs." If we cannot move away from "principles and declarations" and toward "concrete devices and mechanisms to alter incentives" and thus achieve true "global collective action," as Esty and Ivanova demand, then we must face the sad likelihood that the well-intentioned plethora of arrangements will yield merely a continuation of today's unsatisfactory progress.

Daniel C. Esty holds faculty appointments at both the School of Forestry and Environmental Studies and the Law School at Yale University. He is the director of the Yale Center for Environmental Law and Policy and of the recently launched Yale World Fellows Program. He is the author or editor of six books and numerous articles on environmental policy issues and the relationships between the environment and trade, security, competitiveness, international institutions, and development. Esty has served in a variety of positions at the U.S. Environmental Protection Agency, including Deputy Assistant Administrator for Policy. Before moving to Yale, he was a senior fellow at the Institute for International Economics in Washington.

Maria H. Ivanova is the director of the Global Environmental Governance Project at the Yale Center for Environmental Law and Policy. Her work focuses on options for strengthening international environmental institutions to better respond to global-scale challenges. A Bulgarian national, she is currently a doctoral candidate at the Yale School of Forestry and Environmental Studies. Ivanova has worked at the Environment Directorate of the Organization for Economic Cooperation and Development (OECD) and the Swedish Environmental Protection Agency on environmental regulatory reform and water quality standards in the newly independent states of the former Soviet Union.

—J.G.S.

CHAPTER 5

Toward a Global Environmental Mechanism

Daniel C. Esty and Maria H. Ivanova

From thinning of the ozone layer to depleted fisheries, to the possibility of climate change, the world community faces today a number of inherently global challenges. Advances in a range of ecological sciences continue to unveil new threats to the "global commons" that deserve attention—from airborne mercury to disrupted hydrological systems—as well as new interrelationships among issues. Yet, the disconnect between needs and performance in the current international environmental regime is striking.

Devised during the infancy of environmental awareness when problems were perceived as largely local, relatively distinct, and subject to technological fixes, the international environmental regime is weak, fragmented, and lacking in resources and authority. A web of over five hundred international environmental agreements has been created over the last thirty years supported by dozens of separate secretariats and institutions. Yet the downward environmental trends continue in many areas. Some of the current failings can be attributed to a history of management shortcomings and bureaucratic entanglements, but other aspects of the problem are deeper and more structural. Governments have failed to create a strong, vibrant institutional architecture for the management of ecological interdependence. The fact that other global challenges—international economic affairs, population growth, and various world health problems (e.g., eradication of polio and smallpox)—have been addressed more successfully is notable.

New institutional mechanisms for global environmental governance are urgently needed. In this chapter, we examine the rationale for reform of the existing global environmental regime and take up three key questions: Do we need environmental efforts at the global scale? Where has the existing system fallen short? What would an effective institutional mechanism for addressing global environmental problems look like?

Our central argument is that there exists today a set of inescapably global environmental threats that require international "collective action." They demand an institutional mechanism at the global level, we argue, but one quite different from traditional international bodies. We propose not a new international bureaucracy but rather the creation of a global environmental mechanism (GEM) that draws on Information Age technologies and networks to promote cooperation in a lighter, faster, more modern and effective manner. To be successful, this new institutional mechanism must alter the incentives facing governments and other stakeholders and facilitate greater cooperation in the provision of global environmental public goods. The GEM must therefore provide adequate information that can help to track trends, highlight issues, characterize the problems to be addressed, provide analysis and policy options, and facilitate agreement on coordinated intervention. It should create a policy "space" for environmental negotiation and bargaining. It should also ensure the sustained buildup of capacity at the international, national, and local scales to address the pressing issues of pollution control and natural resource management.

Rationale for Global Action

The need for international cooperation to address environmental problems with transboundary or global implications is clear both in theory and in practice. Some environmental problems (e.g., local air and water pollution) are of limited geographic scope and can be handled at the national scale. An increasingly large set of issues, however, from persistent organic pollutants to fisheries depletion to climate change, demand an effective response among several jurisdictions and sometimes even coordinated action across the globe. Governments around the world are beginning to recognize their inability to tackle the many environmental problems with international implications on their own. Thus, stronger national, state/regional, and local environmental performance is necessary, but cannot substitute for appropriate action at the global scale.

The solutions to environmental problems represent classic public goods. While markets are the primary producers of private goods, which are delivered to individual buyers, public goods confer benefits that cannot be confined to a single individual or group. Once provided, many can enjoy them for free. Clean air and an intact ozone layer are stark examples. The challenge public goods pose is that, unless carefully managed, they trigger behavior that is individually rational but collectively suboptimal or even disastrous. Since the very nature of public goods is their nonexcludability, rational individuals may choose to "free ride" on the efforts of others rather than contribute resources to the provision of the good in question. For example, it is rational and logical for a fisherman to try to maximize his personal gain by catching as many fish as possible as quickly as possible. Collectively, however, such a strategy would lead to what Garrett Hardin has termed a "tragedy of the commons." The fish stock will be depleted, leaving the entire fishing community worse off than if it had found a cooperative arrangement controlling the rate at which the resources are extracted. Similarly, in a world of multiple governing authorities and jurisdictions, optimal pollution reduction is unlikely to occur without some structure to promote collaboration.

The problem of collective action is especially acute where pollution harms spill across national boundaries (creating what Dua and Esty call "superexternalities") or where the shared resources of the global commons are at issue. At the national level, a regulatory agency is usually given authority to direct (and coerce if need be) the behavior of private actors so as to ensure cooperation. In the absence of an overarching authority at the global level, incentives to free ride are even stronger. To use the example of the fishing community again, even if local members could reach an agreement to regulate catch, the tragedy of the commons will persevere without oversight and control over *foreign* commercial fleets. Crucial fisheries have indeed collapsed worldwide as heavily subsidized fleets sweep ocean floors around the world. In the face of such competition, local fishermen are forced to behave "rationally." In the words of a Mexican fisherman, "The philosophy is, get it now; grab it—if I don't, the next guy will."

Global collective action is further hampered by the spatial scale and temporal diffusion of international environmental issues. Impacts of externalized harms are hard to see, shifting the costs and benefits to other jurisdictions and even other generations. In the case of climate change, for example, the abatement and adaptation costs can be transferred not only spatially—to other countries—but also intertemporally—to future generations. Cooperation is also difficult to obtain when there is a lack of "reciprocity" among the parties involved. Upstream users of a shared river, for instance, have little incentive to limit their extraction of water or curb pollution because the costs they impose will largely be borne by others downstream. And the problems are not just environmental. Economic integration has transformed environmental protection from a clearly domestic issue into one of inherently international scope. In a world of liberalized trade, where the competition for market share is global, the focus has shifted from lowering tariffs to the elimination of nontariff barriers to trade. Since many domestic regulations can potentially be construed as nontariff barriers, the extent and impact of regulatory discipline has expanded, increasing the potential for conflict among national policies. Public health standards, food safety requirements, emissions limits, waste management and disposal rules, and labeling policies all may shape trade flows. Trade disciplines may also affect national-scale environmental efforts, especially to the extent that the dispute settlement procedures of the World Trade Organization (WTO) are used to challenge pollution control or natural resource management programs. With new issues such as biotechnology and climate change emerging, the potential for significant and divisive battles between trade policy and regulatory choices—including environmental rules—looms large. For example, serious attempts to regulate greenhouse gas emissions may radically alter the price of fossil fuels and thus affect the value of hundreds of billions of dollars in industrial assets and energy investments. Similarly, efforts to take more seriously the need to protect biodiversity or to expand the linkage between the trade regime and the Convention on International Trade in Endangered Species (CITES) might also lead to future conflict. In the absence of a functioning global environmental management system capable of addressing trade and environment issues, much of the responsibility for integrating these two policy realms inevitably falls to the WTO. Although the WTO has a Committee on Trade and Environment that has been meeting for several years, the committee is dominated by trade experts, has demonstrated little understanding of the trade effects on environmental policy, and has almost nothing in the way of results to show for its first four years of efforts.

Leaders of the trade community recognize the lack of capacity of the WTO to address conflicting environmental issues effectively and see its efficacy and legitimacy undermined whenever it is forced to make decisions that go beyond the scope of its trade mandate and expertise. Both the recent WTO director-general, Renato Ruggiero, and the incoming director-general, Supachai Panitchpakdi, have called for a concerted effort to strengthen existing bridges between trade and environmental policies. They urged the creation of a World Environment Organization to help focus and coordinate worldwide environmental efforts, thereby relieving environmental pressures on the WTO. Thus, while environmental advocates want to see a global environmental body as a counterweight to the WTO, many trade officials see it as a useful way of unburdening the trade system of global-scale environmental decision-making responsibilities that it is ill-equipped to handle. Most recently, French Prime Minister Lionel Jospin called for the creation of a global environmental organization that would bring greater balance to a multilateral system excessively focused on the economy.[1] Similar calls have come from Mikhail Gorbachev, Jacques Chirac, *The Economist* magazine, and others.

Evaluating Global Environmental Governance

The last three decades have witnessed an outpouring of international environmental activities and activism. The principal focus, however, has been on drafting treaties. Talk has rarely been translated into action. Thus, the downward environmental trends noticed by scientists twenty years ago continue mostly unabated, with ozone depletion as a notable exception as Gus Speth notes in Chapter 1. From halting efforts to understand and confront the prospects of climate change, to the inability to respond to questions about food made with genetically modified organisms, dissatisfaction among politicians, business people, environmentalists, and the general public abounds. Some of the setbacks can be ascribed to management deficiencies and bureaucratic entanglements, but other aspects of the problem are deeper and more structural.

Collective action in the environmental domain has fallen short as a result of the deep-seated weakness of the institutional architecture and decision-making processes of the existing international environmental regime. Fragmentation, gaps in issue coverage, and even contradictions among different treaties, organizations, and agencies with environmental responsibilities have undermined effective, results-oriented action. As pointed out by Charnovitz, "[l]ike a city that does not have zoning ordinances, environmental governance spreads out in unplanned, incongruent, and inefficient ways." A pervasive lack of data, information, and very limited policy transparency adds to the challenge.

Fundamentally, the focus and design of the United Nations Environment Programme (UNEP) predates a full appreciation of the international scope of pollution issues. Hampered by a narrow mandate, a modest budget, and limited political support, the UNEP competes on the international environmental scene with more than a dozen other U.N. bodies, including

---

[1]For the text of the speeches, see Ruggiero 1998; Panitchpakdi 2001; Jospin 2002. For arguments in favor of a World/Global Environment Organization, see Esty 1994, 2000, 2000a; Biermann 2000; Whalley and Zissimos 2001; Runge 2001; Charnovitz 2002. For the opposing view, see Von Moltke 2001; Juma 2000.

the Commission on Sustainable Development (CSD), the U.N. Development Programme (UNDP), the World Meteorological Organization (WMO), and the International Oceanographic Commission (IOC). Adding to this fragmentation are the independent secretariats to numerous treaties, including the Montreal Protocol (ozone layer protection), the Basel Convention (hazardous waste trade), the Convention on International Trade in Endangered Species (CITES), and the Climate Change Convention, all contending for limited governmental time, attention, and resources.

In a recent report, the UNEP's executive director recognized that "[f]rom a combined global and regional perspective, the resultant proliferation of MEAs [multilateral environmental agreements] has placed an increasing burden on Parties and member states to meet their collective obligations and responsibilities to implement environmental conventions and related international agreements." To illustrate this point, one needs only to observe that UNEP, CSD, UNDP, WMO, as well as the Organization for Economic Cooperation and Development (OECD) and the World Bank, all have climate change programs underway with little coordination and no sense of strategic division of labor. When similar treaty congestion threatened to break down international efforts to regulate intellectual property, a single body, the World Intellectual Property Organization, was launched to consolidate global-scale efforts and achieve scale economies in management. The environmental regime faces a similar pressing need for streamlining and coherence.

The existing international environmental system has failed to adequately deal with the priorities of both developed and developing countries. The inadequacy and dispersion of the existing financial mechanisms—scattered across the Global Environmental Facility, U.N. Development Programme, World Bank, and separate funds such as the Montreal Protocol Finance Mechanism—reinforces the perception of a lack of seriousness in the North about the plight of the South. There is also a pervasive suspicion among developing countries of "environmental conditionality." They remain convinced that efforts to advance global-scale environmental standards provide a guise for protectionism. These nations see themselves being blocked from northern markets by nontariff barriers or having their market access limited because they failed to adhere to the North's strict, costly standards. Furthermore, fundamental principles of good governance such as fair representation, transparency, and accountability are still at issue in many of the institutions with environmental responsibilities. These procedural shortcomings undermine the legitimacy of the system as a whole.

A multi-prong agenda of refinements and reform of the UNEP and the other elements of the current international environmental system could be developed to address these many issues. But the list of problems is so long and the baggage associated with the current regime is so heavy that, at some point, a fundamental restructuring rather than incremental tinkering becomes a better path forward. In the face of so many difficulties and the existing regime's poor track record, any presumption in favor of working with the status quo cannot be sustained. Moreover, as the analysis above suggests, the nub of the issue is structural, making a different starting point and a new institutional design advisable.

Global Environmental Mechanism

To effectively respond to both the common elements of national problems and the special demands of transboundary issues, a new global environmental mechanism (GEM) is needed. Conceptually, a GEM fills an undeniable need for a mechanism to promote collective action at the international scale. Practically, it offers the chance to build a coherent and integrated environmental policymaking and management framework that addresses the challenges of a shared global ecosystem.

We see three core capacities as essential to a GEM: (1) the provision of adequate information that can help to characterize the problems to be addressed, reveal preferences, and alter interests; (2) the creation of a policy "space" for environmental negotiation and bargaining; and (3) the sustained buildup of capacity for addressing issues of concern and significance. We identify data collection, monitoring, scientific assessment, and analysis as central in the information domain. A forum for issue linkages and bargaining, a mechanism for rule making, and a dispute settlement framework are essential to ensuring cooperative solutions. The development of technical, financial, human, and institutional capacity for addressing diverse challenges is another critical function demanding effective institutional mechanisms at the global level. Figure 5-1 illustrates the functions and mechanisms we deem necessary at the global level.

Various institutions and agencies are currently performing many of the identified capacities. Others are flagrantly absent. For example, a suite of international organizations, scientific research centers, national governments, and environmental convention secretariats are carrying out data collection, scientific assessment, financing, and technology transfer, albeit with little coordination and poor comparability across jurisdictions. Compliance monitoring and reporting are unsystematic, scattered,

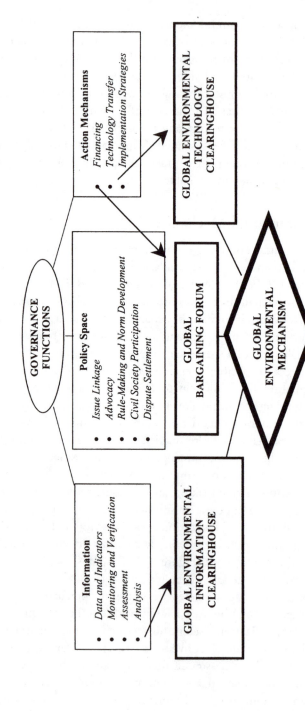

Figure 5-1. Governance Functions.

and largely informal. The modalities for participation of nonstate actors require further elaboration and institutionalization along with procedures for rule making. A forum for issue linkage, bargaining, and trade-offs and a dispute settlement mechanism are lacking. Moreover, a stronger policy space for the environment is necessary to sustain efforts at environmental advocacy within the broader system of global governance and to ensure that environmental concerns are integrated into sustainable development policies.

Building on the expertise and capacities of existing institutions and creating new mechanisms where functions are currently unfulfilled, we envision the following institutional mechanisms as comprising the GEM:

- *Data Collection Mechanism.* Ensuring the availability of reliable data of high quality and comparability, developing indicators and benchmarks, and publishing "State of the Global Environment" reports.
- *Compliance Monitoring and Reporting Mechanism.* Providing a repository for information on compliance and a continuous and transparent reporting effort.
- *Scientific Assessment and Knowledge Networking Mechanism.* Performing basic research on environmental processes and trends, long-term forecasting, and early warnings of environmental risks.
- *Bargaining and Trade-Offs Mechanism.* Facilitating the internalization of externalities through exchanges of commitments on various environmental issues (forest cover, biodiversity protection, species management, etc.) in return for cash or policy change (market access).
- *Rule-Making Mechanism.* For the global commons, establishing policy guidelines and international norms on protection of shared global resources.
- *Civil Society Participation Mechanism.* Providing a business and NGO forum for direct participation in problem identification and policy formulation.
- *Financing Mechanism.* For global-scale issues, mobilizing both public and private resources to provide structured financial assistance to developing countries and transition economies.
- *Technology Transfer Mechanism.* Promoting the adoption of best options suited to national conditions and encouraging innovative local solutions.
- *Dispute Settlement Mechanism.* With agreed procedures and rules to promote conflict resolution between environmental agreements and vis-à-vis other global governance regimes in an equitable manner.
- *Implementation Strategies Mechanism.* Ensuring coordination with institutions with primary implementation responsibility (e.g., national

governments, UNDP, World Bank, business, civil society organizations) and providing a database of best practices.

GLOBAL ENVIRONMENTAL INFORMATION CLEARINGHOUSE

Sound decision making hinges on the availability of data and information. High-quality data with cross-country comparability is necessary to support an integrated, ecosystem-based approach to problem definition and assessment. Currently, the mandate to collect, assess, and disseminate data is divided among a multitude of agencies, and there is little coordination among the various efforts. The UNEP has established an Environment and Natural Resources Information Network to help collate, store, manage, and disseminate environmental information and data in developing countries and to assess environment and development issues for decision making, policy setting, and planning. The UNDP has launched a similar initiative with its Capacity 21 program. The multiple convention secretariats are also responsible for assembling and analyzing data. A global information clearinghouse could provide an important mechanism for the alteration of interests and incentives. Reliable information on risks and trends could alert to the need for action. Comparable data on performance (similar to the national PROPER scheme in Indonesia) could provide much greater transparency, reward the leaders, and expose the laggards, encouraging a shift in behavior. The attention that the World Economic Forum's Environmental Sustainability Index has generated shows the potential. While data gathering should primarily be the function of national, local, or even international organizations, a central repository for such information and a mechanism for making the information publicly available would represent a significant discipline on slack performance. An information clearinghouse will not, in reality, centralize science policy *functions* but create, as a 2002 U.N. University report notes, a "centralized source for coordinating information flow between the institutions responsible for performing the different science policy functions."

GLOBAL ENVIRONMENTAL TECHNOLOGY CLEARINGHOUSE

At the local, national, and global levels, several aspects of capacity development need to be emphasized. Technical, financial, human, and institutional capabilities are all critical to sound environmental policy. The process of selecting and operating environmentally sound technologies, for example, is not as simple and straightforward as it is sometimes believed. Selecting a technology that is suitable for local needs, adapting it to local conditions, and maintaining it requires substantial skills and information. The existing institutional mechanisms for technology transfer have been less than effective. The tying of technology transfer to official aid and export promotion policies has often resulted in the imposition of inappropriate technologies on countries with little capacity to choose, assess, operate, and maintain them. It has in turn led to suspicion on the part of developing countries and a reference to the CDM (Clean Development Mechanism) as the "Convenient Dumping Mechanism" by skeptics of the approach. The limited access to information and the limited technical capacity of the recipients of technology underscore the need for a clearinghouse on various abatement technologies.

An environmental technology clearinghouse could serve as the repository and disseminator of information facilitating active participation in the process of choosing and assessing the appropriate technologies. It could also encompass information on best practices around the world that would ensure continuous learning. The clearinghouse will thus be critical to the creation of technological and innovation capabilities in recipient countries. It could address the need, as Malik Aslam writes, "to work out a collaborative model between the North and the South that can cater to both the soft and the hard aspects of technology transfer, be driven by local needs, adapted to the developing country operational environment and sustained through facilitated private sector participation."

GLOBAL BARGAINING FORUM

A key function of global environmental governance should be the provision of incentives for the internalization of international externalities. However, the international discourse in the past decade has focused on principles and negotiations rather than operational mechanisms to improve environmental results. Moreover, "environmental negotiations, up to now, have been conducted largely in isolation from negotiations on other international issues such as debt, trade, or security" (Susskind and Ozawa 1992 cited in Runge 2001). Thus, issue linkage has been avoided and a practice of agreeing to lowest-common-denominator treaties has been perpetuated. As elaborated by Whalley and Zissimos (2001, 2002), we see the value in a forum for the facilitation of international deals on the environment that improve quality and result in cash flow to custodians of environmental assets.

A global bargaining forum could act as a catalyst between countries or private entities negotiating the transfer of resources in exchange for commitments to agreed-upon policies and behavior. Thus, a government in one country might negotiate a deal to preserve a particular natural resource—such as a part of a rain forest or a set of species—in another country in return for a sum of money or other policy benefits. For example, market access is an issue of paramount importance to developing country economies and has been used as a condition for any concessions on issues of interest to the North. Brazil has made a market access agreement in agriculture a precondition to its involvement in a new trade negotiations round. India has made commitments on intellectual property rights in exchange for expanded market access in agriculture and textiles. A global bargaining forum could allow such deals to be negotiated and ensure that incentives are altered, leading to higher environmental quality, and that new resources flow to developing countries that are usually the stewards of many global public goods.[2] The forum, however, also needs to comprise a set of mechanisms for verification, financial transfers, and potential dispute settlement.

In proposing a loosely structured GEM, we emphasize the need for form to follow function. We envision a "light" institutional superstructure providing coordination through a staff comparable to the WTO secretariat in Geneva. The secretariat would help to promote cooperation and achieve synergies across the disparate multilateral environmental agreements and other international institutions with environmental roles. It would also act as a mediator and buffer between the environment and the Bretton Woods institutions with their economic focus. The GEM would thus neither add a new layer of international bureaucracy nor create a world government. Quite to the contrary, movement toward a GEM should entail consolidation of the existing panoply of international environmental institutions and a shift toward a more modern "virtual" organizational structure.

At the center of our proposal for a GEM lies a global public policy network, drawing in issue-specific expertise from around the world. Such a network, drawing on an established set of private and public organizations with environmental expertise, can operate as a flexible system for advancing international environmental agenda-setting, analysis, negotiation, policy formulation, implementation, and institutional learning. The benefits of such a structure are increasingly clear. Global public policy and issue networks represent an innovative organizational mechanism for responding to

---

[2]For a detailed argument on the need for an international forum for issue linkage and bargaining, see Whalley and Zissimos 2001, 2002.

an ever more complex international policy environment, taking advantage of Information Age communications and information technologies to build new opportunities for cooperation.[3]

A more streamlined environmental regime with a small hub and a largely virtual structure would be especially beneficial to the South. In particular, a single venue for negotiations and international coordination would make it much easier for the overstretched environment ministries of the developing world to monitor the spectrum of environmental issues at play and to contribute thoughtfully to the global-scale debate even with a relatively small international policymaking team. There would be no need to traipse around the world trying to keep up with the plethora of separate bodies and meetings. A "network" approach drawing in diverse perspectives and expertise and using the Internet could facilitate greater developing country participation in the international policy-making process.

A second issue of particular importance to developing countries involves who will pay for global-scale environmental problem solving. By placing the principle of common but differentiated responsibilities at the center of the new mechanism along with a real forum for bargaining and trade-offs, efforts to strike a fair balance of rights and responsibilities with regard to transboundary environmental issues might be improved. A more carefully considered and coherent set of international environmental standards would also alleviate fears in the South that the industrialized world seeks to impose unreasonably high standards (and perhaps trade penalties for noncompliance) on developing countries, all of whom have many competing demands for limited public resources. Moreover, mechanisms to support technology transfers and to subsidize developing country environmental initiatives in pursuit of global environmental goals would help to alleviate North–South tensions.

A related question is whose values will be promoted in a strengthened international environmental regime. Such concerns make it essential that a GEM be seen as a transparent and inclusive forum that seeks to build consensus on a basis that respects the diversity of views across the world. It

---

[3]Examples of successful public policy networks include the *The World Commission on Dams* (recently awarded the highest environmental recognition, the Zayed International Prize for the Environment, for effectively addressing the environmental impacts of large dams and setting a standard for other complex environmental problems), *The Global Knowledge Partnership,* and the *Roll Back Malaria* initiative. For more information on these and other public policy networks, see http://www.yale.edu/gegdialogue/morepublicpolicynetwork.html.

should also be noted that properly managed public policy networks create "virtual public space" that is easier to enter than the established physical fora where decisions are currently made. An Information Age set of outreach mechanisms could also decrease the distance between decentralized constituencies and global decision makers—making it easier to insert into the policy process the broad array of values, perceptions, and perspectives that are now often overlooked or incompletely considered, and facilitating public understanding of the issues being addressed and decisions being made at the global scale.

Conclusion

Global environmental policymaking in the last decade has focused exclusively on principles and declarations rather than concrete devices and mechanisms to alter incentives. The global environmental management system is clearly falling short of both the world community's needs and its expectations. It is time to reengineer the regime, aiming for a new, forward-looking, sleeker, and more efficient architecture that will better serve environmental, governmental, public, and business needs. The logic of a global environmental mechanism is straightforward: a globalizing world requires thoughtful and modern ways to manage ecological interdependence. A vibrant and focused new institutional structure could provide the data foundation needed for good environmental decision making; a capacity to gauge risks, costs, benefits, and policy options comparatively; a mechanism for leveraging private sector and governmental resources deployed at the international level; and a means for improving results from global-scale environmental spending and programs. The world community would benefit from the presence of an authoritative environmental voice in the international arena and a recognized forum for national officials and other stakeholders to work cooperatively to address global issues.

An extraordinary mix of political idealism and pragmatism will be required to launch a GEM. One approach would be to start modestly and have the new mechanism grow into its mandate over time. Scientific activities represent the dimension of the policy realm where scale economies and other efficiency gains can most quickly be realized from increased cooperation. Thus, an "Information Initiative" could become the first concrete step toward the establishment of a GEM. The coordination of existing institutional mechanisms for data collection, scientific assessment, and analysis might attract broad-based support. A "Technology Initiative," focusing on information sharing and best-practices dissemination, might also be launched as an early GEM element. With its competence established in these areas, the GEM mandate might then be expanded to include monitoring, rule making, and the development of a bargaining forum. Subsequently, the GEM might acquire a dispute settlement mechanism.

More broadly, a commitment to revitalize the international environmental regime should be cast as part of a wider "global bargain." Specifically, the launch of a GEM needs to be paired with a major new poverty alleviation initiative (driven through an invigorated World Bank and UNDP).

References

Aslam, Malik Amin. 2001. Technology Transfer under the CDM: Materializing the Myth in the Japanese Context? *Climate Policy* (1):451–464.

Biermann, Frank. 2000. The Case for a World Environment Organization. *Environment* 42(9):22.

Charnovitz, Steven. 2002. A World Environment Organization. *Columbia Journal of Environmental Law* (Forthcoming).

Dua, Andre, and Daniel C. Esty. 1997. *Sustaining the Asian Pacific Miracle: Economic Integration and Environmental Protection.* Washington, D.C.: Institute for International Economics.

ESI. 2002. Environmental Sustainability Index. Davos, Switzerland: World Economic Forum, available at http://www.yale.edu/envirocenter/esi.

Esty, Daniel C. 1994. *Greening the GATT: Trade, Environment, and the Future.* Washington, D.C.: Institute for International Economics.

———. 1999. Economic Integration and the Environment. In *The Global Environment: Institutions, Law, and Policy,* edited by N. J. Vig and R. S. Axelrod. Washington, D.C.: CQ Press.

———. 2000. Stepping Up to the Global Environmental Challenge. *Fordham Environmental Law Journal* 8(1):103–113.

———. 2000a. Global Environmental Agency Will Take Pressure Off WTO. *Financial Times,* July 13, 2000.

Esty, Daniel C., and Peter Cornelius, eds. 2002. *Environmental Performance Measurement: The Global Report 2001–2002.* New York: Oxford University Press.

Esty, Daniel C., and Maria Ivanova. 2001. Making International Environmental Agreements Work: The Case for a Global Environmental Organization. *Yale Center for Environmental Law and Policy Working Papers Series.* Working Paper 2/1, May 2001 (available at http://www.yale.edu/gegdialogue).

Hardin, Garrett. 1968. The Tragedy of the Commons. *Science* 162:1243.

Jospin, Lionel. 2002. French Prime Minister Calls for Creation Of New World Environment Organization. *International Environment Reporter* 25(5):213.

Juma, Calestous. 2000. The Perils of Centralizing Global Environmental Governance. In *Environment Matters, Annual Review.* Washington, D.C.: The World Bank.

Kaul, Inge. 2001. Public Goods in the 21st Century. In *Global Public Goods: Taking the Concept Forward,* edited by M. Faust, I. Kaul, K. Le Goulven, G. Ryu, and

M. Schnupf. New York: UNDP Office of Development Studies, Discussion Paper Series.

Panitchpakdi, H.E. Dr. Supachai. 2001. Keynote Address: The Evolving Multilateral Trade System in the New Millennium. *George Washington University International Law Review* 33:419–443.

Ruggiero, Renato. 1998. A Global System for the Next Fifty Years. Address to the Royal Institute of International Affairs.

Runge, C. Ford. 2001. A Global Environmental Organization (GEO) and the World Trading System. *Journal of World Trade* 35(4):399–426.

Susskind, Lawrence, and Connie Ozawa. 1992. Negotiating More Effective International Environmental Agreements. In *The International Politics of the Environment: Actors, Interests, and Institutions,* edited by A. Hurrell and B. Kingsbury. Oxford: Clarendon Press.

UNEP. 2001. International Environmental Governance: Report of the Executive Director. Nairobi: United Nations Environment Programme (UNEP).

U.N. University. 2002. International Environmental Governance. The Question of Reform: Key Issues and Proposals. Preliminary Findings. Tokyo: United Nations University Institute for Advanced Studies.

Von Moltke, Konrad. 2001. The Organization of the Impossible. *Global Environmental Politics* 1(1).

Weiner, Tim. 2002. In Mexico, Greed Kills Fish by the Seaful. *New York Times,* April 10, 2002.

Whalley, John, and Ben Zissimos. 2001. What Could a World Environmental Organization Do? *Global Environmental Politics* 1(1).

———. 2002. Economic Underpinnings of Global Environmental Governance: The Need for a New Authority. In *Global Environmental Governance: Options and Opportunities in an Interdependent World,* edited by D. C. Esty and M. Ivanova. New Haven, Conn.: Yale School of Forestry & Environmental Studies.

Young, Oran R. 1999. *The Effectiveness of International Environmental Regimes: Causal Connections and Behavioral Mechanisms.* Cambridge, Mass.: MIT Press.

Introduction

Robert Kates examines the "genius of the oxymoron of sustainable development that lies in its essential ambiguity," one that "seeks to finesse the real conflicts between economy and environment and between the present and the future." In looking at the successes and failures of past and contemporary globalization, Kates concludes that while globalization has allowed the world community to attack certain problems effectively, to date its harms have overwhelmed its benefits. "[G]lobalization has not helped reduce the numbers of chronically hungry in the world. . . . The shifts in investment, income, and job opportunities in some parts of the world are matched by the growth of hunger elsewhere. . . . [D]espite major gains in technologies that reduce the use of energy and materials per unit of production, the absolute growth in consumption overwhelms the steady global technological progress." Kates argues, however, that those of us who aspire to a transition toward sustainability, to meet human needs while preserving the life support of the planet, cannot be "against globalization."

He advances the idea that just as capitalism was (over a century) "civilized" through the rule of law, increased transparency, and the creation of better forms of governance, so must globalization be—the difference being that this change must be compressed into perhaps the next two decades, and that its best hope now comes from the "bottom up," through the popular movements and groups that are now well advanced in their efforts to "humanize" globalization.

Dr. Robert Kates is a geographer who served as the first director of the Feinstein World Hunger Program at Brown University until his retirement in 1992. In 1991, he was awarded the National Medal of Science for his work on hunger, environment, and natural hazards. He played a major role in the completion of the National Academy of Sciences report *Our Common Journey: A Transition toward Sustainability.* He is a member of the National Academy of Sciences and the American Academy of Arts and Sciences and is a visiting scholar at the Belfer Center for Science and International Affairs at Harvard University's Kennedy School of Government. Currently, Kates serves as co-convenor of the Initiative on Science and Technology for Sustainability, is executive editor of *Environment* magazine, and is University Professor emeritus at Brown University. He now continues his work as an independent scholar from his home in Maine.

—J.G.S.

CHAPTER 6

The Nexus and the Neem Tree: Globalization and a Transition toward Sustainability

Robert W. Kates

The world of this new century is in transition—becoming more crowded and more consuming, warmer and more stressed, more interconnected, yet diverse and divided. Can this transition also be a transition for sustainability, in which the more than 9 billion people of the next half century meet their wants and needs in ways that do not further degrade the planet's life-support systems?

In this chapter, I explore this transition to sustainability, the context in which it will take place, and the ways in which the new-old phenomenon of globalization affects it. My title is a play on the title of what may be the best-known book on globalization—Tom Friedman's *The Lexus and the Olive Tree.*

Friedman describes his title as follows:

> So there I was speeding along at 180 miles an hour on the most modern train in the world, reading this story about the oldest corner of the world. And the thought occurred to me that these Japanese, whose Lexus factory I had just visited and whose train I was riding, were building the greatest luxury car in the world with robots. And over here, on the top of page 3 of the *Herald Tribune,* the people with whom I had lived for so many years in Beirut and Jerusalem, whom I knew so well, were still fighting over who owned which olive tree. It struck me then that the Lexus and the olive tree were pretty good symbols of this post–Cold War era: half the world seemed to be emerging from the Cold War intent on building a better Lexus, dedicated to modernizing, streamlining and privatizing their economies in

order to thrive in the system of globalization. And half the world—sometimes half the same country, sometimes half the same person—was still caught up in the fight over who owns which olive tree (p. 31).

But unlike this Lexus, which stands for all that is modern and different in globalization, and the olive tree for all that resists it, the nexus I explore is that of environment and development and the context in which it will play out over the coming two generations. And the Neem tree symbolizes the globalizing world where the elements of both the Lexus and the olive tree coexist in an uneasy tension of mutual attraction and repulsion.

I use three critical goals required for a successful sustainability transition—meeting human needs, reducing hunger and poverty, and preserving the life-support systems of the planet—to ask how globalization might help or hinder achieving these. For globalization to help more than hinder, it will need to be "civilized," and I conclude with an analog of how that might take place.

Sustainable Development: The Nexus of Environment and Development

The nexus of society's developmental goals with its environmental limits over the long term comes together in "sustainable development," which is only the most recent effort to link together the collective aspirations of the peoples of the world. Over my adult life, four aspirations emerged: first, for peace in the postwar world of 1945; then for freedom, in the struggles in the late 1940s and 1950s to end imperialism; followed by development for the poorest three-fourths of the world; and last, in the final quarter of the century, a concern for a healthy environment for humankind, the earth itself, and its complex systems that support life. As global aspirations develop, good people try to bring them together in a characteristic pattern of international high-level commissions (Brandt, Palme, Brundtland), followed by great international conferences. Such was the 1987 report of the World Commission on Environment and Development (WCED, also known as the Brundtland Commission) widely disseminated as *Our Common Future* (WCED, 1987), followed by the United Nations Conference on Environment and Development (UNCED) in Rio de Janeiro in 1992, and now a decade later in South Africa as the World Summit for Sustainable Development.

"Sustainable development" is now central to the mission of countless international organizations, national institutions, "sustainable cities" and locales, transnational corporations, and nongovernmental organizations. The genius of the oxymoron of sustainable development lies in its essential ambiguity that seeks to finesse the real conflicts between economy and environment and between the present and the future. While sharing a common concern for the fate of the earth, proponents of sustainable development differ in their emphases on what is to be sustained, what is to be developed, how to link environment and development, and for how long a time (see Figure 6-1). Thus, proponents differ on what is to be sustained: Is it nature itself, or nature in the utilitarian life support of humankind, and does it include sustaining the community of the olive tree, as Friedman (2000) describes it: "everything that roots us . . . family, a community, a tribe, a nation, a religion or, most of all, a place called home" (p. 31)? Proponents differ on what is to be developed: Is it the economy, some broader notion of society, or is it people themselves? And how shall we link the two: sustain only, develop mostly, develop only but sustain somewhat, sustain or develop?—these and many more permutations are found. Finally, over what time horizon will this occur? The Bruntland report employs the

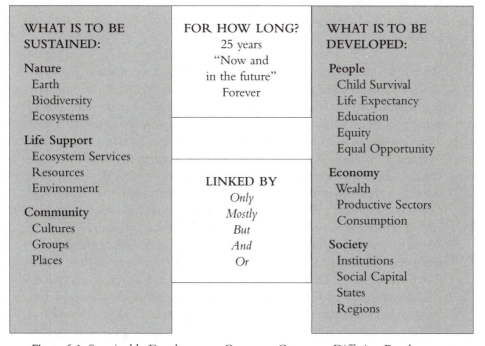

Figure 6-1. Sustainable Development: Common Concerns, Differing Emphases.

usefully ambiguous and widely accepted time horizon as "now and in the future." But in a future of a single generation, twenty-five years, almost any development appears sustainable. Over an infinite forever, none does, as even the smallest growth extended indefinitely creates situations that seem surely unsustainable. And over the century, now encompassed in many assessments such as that of climate change, the large and the long future is both remote and uncertain.

While a major political success, sustainable development has not been a significant scientific focus beyond the earliest days of its conceptualization. While originating in the scientific activities of the early 1980s, particularly the work of the International Union for the Conservation of Nature (IUCN), as sustainable development gained greater political adherence, organized science found less to address. This has now changed, and a focus on a transition toward sustainability has made sustainable development scientifically manageable, and measurable for the world academies of science (IAP, 2000), for the international organizations of science (ICSU/WFEO, 2002), and increasingly for an emergent sustainability science (Kates et al., 2001).

In 1995, the Board on Sustainable Development of the U.S. National Academy of Sciences–National Research Council (NAS-NRC) sought to resolve some of the ambiguity I have described by focusing on a transition to sustainability over the next fifty years. By focusing on a transition, we took as our starting point the best understood of future trends—the demographic transition from a world with a population that grew by many births and many deaths to one that stabilized with few births and few deaths. With such a transition well under way, we can with some confidence project a declining or steady state population by the end of this century, with the bulk of that population born by 2050 (perhaps 9 billion of an eventual 10 billion). Thus, the human development needs of that population will surely increase, compared to the more than 6 billion alive today, but probably not more than by half again as much as that of today. The board defined a sustainability transition as one that would meet the human needs for food, nurture, housing, education, and employment of that larger but finite population, significantly reducing hunger and poverty, while still maintaining the essential life-support systems of the planet (NRC-BSD, 1999). These human needs are unmet today; for example, in 1995, 16 percent of the world population was hungry, 24 percent had unsafe water to drink, and 24 percent were illiterate (Raskin et al., 1998).

For these three normative goals, we found ample consensual support and measurable targets in the deliberations and subsequent treaties of international conferences and summits of leaders. For example, for the amount of reduction in hunger and poverty we used international consensus statements that call for reducing hunger and poverty by half within one to two decades (IMF et al., 2002) and suggested a target of reducing hunger by half in each of the next two generations.

Compared to meeting human needs, quantitative targets for preserving life-support systems are fewer, more modest, and more contested. Global targets now exist for reducing ozone-depleting substances, greenhouse gases, and, regionally, for some air pollutants. Absolute prohibitions (zero targets) exist for ocean dumping of radioactive wastes and some toxics (persistent organic pesticides), for the taking and/or sale of a few large mammals (whales, elephants, seals), migratory birds when breeding or endangered, and certain regional fishing stocks. International standards exist for many toxic materials, organic pollutants, and heavy metals that threaten human health, but not for ecosystem health. Water, land, and vegetative resources, such as arid lands or forests, have at best qualitative aspirations for sustainable management or restoration.

The Neem Tree: The New and Old Globalization

The 1992 NAS-NRC report *Neem: A Tree for Solving Global Problems* begins:

> Neem is a fascinating tree. On the one hand, it seems to be one of the most promising of all plants, and may eventually benefit every person on the planet. Probably no other yields as many strange and varied products or has as many exploitable by-products. Indeed, as foreseen by some scientists, this plant may usher in new era in pest control, provide millions with inexpensive medicines, cut down the rate of human population growth, and perhaps even reduce erosion, deforestation, and the excessive temperature of an overheated globe.

The Neem tree, *Azadirachta indica* (Figure 6-2), is an attractive broad-leafed evergreen that grows tall and broad and can live for a century or more. Native to South Asia, it has been carried over the last century to the rest of tropical and semitropical Asia, Africa, and increasingly to the Caribbean and Central America and is now well established in thirty countries and has been introduced to many more. Everywhere it grows, it is prized for its ability to grow in marginal soils, to provide shade, firewood,

Figure 6-2. Neem Tree.

oil for lamps, cosmetics, soaps, lubrication, and medicinals that date back several millennia, twig toothbrushes that prevent gum disease, and as a natural insecticide. Even where it does not grow, word of its wonders are carried on numerous Web sites, many dedicated to the Neem itself.

But it is for its pesticidal qualities—as a safer alternative to dangerous neurotoxins, effective across a large range of insects, fungi, nematodes, and the like, and seemingly safe for humans, birds, and animals—that Neem has attracted considerable scientific and commercial interest. More than seventy patents for uses or processes related to Neem products exist, and in May 2000 in an important decision, the European Patent Office revoked the patent given to W. R. Grace company for a fungicidal product, a decision hailed by Vandana Shiva (see Chapter 9), who had challenged the original patent, as "a great day for all who have been fighting to take back control of their resources and knowledge-systems from the patent regimes of the North" (Anon. 2000).

Thus, the Neem shares three major characteristics of globalization. It is not new, but quite ancient, as is globalization. In ancient Sanskrit it is known as *aristha,* or reliever of sickness. As with previous globalizations, it spread with religion and with empire. Part of traditional ayurvedic medicine, the Neem is found wherever Hinduism is found and often where the British Empire ruled. But as with globalization, there is much that is new in its dispersal and product development, as Neem seeds are now an international commodity. Modern science is close to synthesizing its major insecticidal properties, international nongovernmental organizations encourage its usage for impoverished rural peoples, and Web sites huckster its cosmetic and medicinal values. Finally, as with globalization, it is full of unrealized promise and currently realized discord. For except as a source of shade, firewood, toothbrushes, oil, or home remedies, it is not widely used beyond its South Asian home; and its most promising commercial products—refined or synthesized and standardized pesticides, medicinals, or contraceptives—are either underdeveloped or contested as to their efficacy and safety, as well as ethically in relation to the commercialization of an ancient legacy of nature and humankind.

Contemporary Globalization

As to globalization in general, I prefer the simplified definition by Held, McGrew, Goldblatt, and Perraton (1999) in *Global Transformations: Politics, Economics, and Culture,* a study that some think is currently the best academic book on the subject. Held et al. say that "in its simplest sense globalization refers to the widening, deepening and speeding up of global interconnectedness . . . " (p. 14). But, of course, as good academics they are not content with such simplicity and go on to describe a set of technical terms and criteria to mirror these items as extensiveness, intensiveness, velocity, and the impacts of interconnections.

Globalization, as noted, is not new, and Held et al. recognize four major periods of globalization: the premodern period of early empires and world religions, the early modern period of Western expansion, the modern industrial era, and the contemporary period from 1945 to the present. I would add two others: the earliest prehistoric period in which humans spread out of Africa around the world, and the future, especially that of the first half of the twenty-first century.

Reviewing the contemporary period and projecting to the future, our academy study (NRC-BSD, 1999) identified some major dimensions of contemporary globalization. The first is global interconnectedness with the much larger population of the future more closely connected by ties of economic production and consumption, migration, communication, and interlinked technologies. Since 1950, trade between nations has grown at more than twice the rate of the economy, and now some 20 percent of the world's goods and services pass over a border. Trade in money and capital—a hundred times the volume of world trade—now moves at a dizzying pace with electronic movement of funds, worldwide currency markets, and twenty-four-hour financial markets.

Words, images, and ideas also outpace the flow of products. New information technologies and mass communication techniques will continue to penetrate many different linguistic, cultural, and political barriers. Flows of people—temporary, permanent, and forced—have also increased, although most movements are poorly measured. The rate of increase in refugees is more rapid than that of world trade.

The rapid movement of peoples and products also makes possible the rapid transmission of infectious diseases of people, crops, and livestock and the biological invasions so destructive of native biota. Environmental harms are exported to countries with weak environmental standards. Most feared of all may be the rapid increases in consumption fueled by aggressive marketing and rapid cultural change. But as communication carries a culture of consumption, it also carries a culture of universal concern with the fate of the earth and links to common international efforts, shared information, and growing numbers of environmental groups.

But the academy study also considered the persistence of diversity, how connectedness, while increasing the similarity of places, can also increase diversity, particularly in urban areas that attract migrants. Places of wealth or opportunity toward which people and products are drawn actually become more diverse. There are also strong countercurrents to global culture that emphasize ethnic, national, and religious distinctiveness.

Finally, connectedness and diversity are also reflected in institutional innovation and power shifts (Mathews, 1997). At a global level, new institutions of governance have emerged, transnational corporate and financial institutions grow and consolidate, and networks of nongovernmental institutions collaborate and expand. At the subnational level, government has devolved, privatization is common, and civic society in many places has been strengthened. Power has shifted from the national state—upward to the global level and downward to the local level—and at all levels from the public to the private.

How does globalization affect a transition toward sustainability in meeting human needs, reducing hunger and poverty, and preserving life-support systems? It helps in some ways, hinders in others, and for many important characteristics, it does both. In this exploration of a highly complex subject, I present two illustrative examples using qualitative, but ordered, judgments. For one, I combine the first two human needs, feeding and nurturing, with the related goal of reducing hunger. In the second, I explore the determinants of threats to the life-support systems.

Feeding, Nurturing, and Reducing Hunger

There are three major types of hunger: chronic household hunger, episodic hunger, and special-needs hunger. Each responds somewhat differently to globalization.

GLOBALIZATION AND REDUCING CHRONIC HUNGER

Current estimates find some 800–900 million people who are chronically hungry—living in households with insufficient income or its equivalent to provide for health, children's growth, and ability to work. The numbers of hungry people differ greatly between regions of the world, with the largest numbers in Asia and the greatest proportion in Africa (Table 6-1).

The number of chronically hungry people can be approximately estimated by using four variables: the size of the population, the average income per person, the distribution of income across the population, and the definition of a hunger line of income, or its equivalent, below which the population is thought to be hungry (see Figure 6-3).

It is useful to examine some differences in these major determinants over the period of contemporary globalization beginning in 1950. World *population* grew over a half century from 2.5 billion to 6 billion, but the

Table 6-1. Numbers and Proportion of Chronically Hungry Population, 1996–1998.

Regions	Hungry Population (millions)	% Total Population
Sub-Saharan Africa	34	186
Near East/North Africa	10	36
Latin America and the Caribbean	11	55
China and India	16	348
Other Asia	19	166
Developing countries: Total	18	791

Source: FAO, 2000.

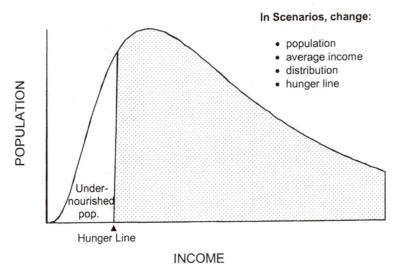

Figure 6-3. Hunger and Income.

peak growth rate was in the 1960s and has been slowing ever since. Nonetheless, about 80 million people are added each year, increasing the numbers of chronically hungry even as the proportion of hungry people diminishes. Examining trends in *income* (Table 6-2) in this period, per capita gross domestic product (GDP) grew in all world regions between 1950 and 1973, but between 1973 and 1992, GDP in Eastern Europe declined, and it stagnated in Africa and Latin America.

Inequality in the *distribution of income* occurs both between countries and regions and within countries and regions. Between regions, Africa, Eastern Europe, and Latin America (Table 6-2) show growing inequality with the United States (ratio of U.S. GDP per capita to regional GDP per capita), even as the rest of Europe converged with the United States and the ratio of U.S per capita GDP to Asia declines from sevenfold in 1973 to fourfold in the course of two decades. Using a different data set (Deininger and Squire, 1996), within-region inequality of income (as measured by the Gini coefficient, a standard measure of inequality) differs almost twofold with the greatest inequality found in Latin America and the least found among the former socialist countries of Eastern Europe. Over time, for most regions, within-region inequality has been generally diminishing except in Africa and in Eastern Europe with the end of socialism. Finally, the *hunger line* grows over time as income increases, access to informal sources of food declines, food purchases increase, and diets change.

The NAS-NRC Board on Sustainable Development commissioned a

Table 6-2. Trends in Regional GDP Per Capita, 1950, 1973, and 1992.

World Regions	1950 GDP/ capita (in 1990 $)	GDP/capita/ 1950 GDP/capita		U.S. GDP/capita/ REGIONAL GDP/capita		
		1973	*1992*	*1950*	*1973*	*1992*
United States	9573	1.7	2.3	1.0	1.0	1.0
Western Europe	5513	2.1	3.2	1.7	1.4	1.2
East Europe	2235	2.4	2.0	4.3	3.1	4.7
Latin America	3478	1.4	1.7	2.8	3.3	3.6
Asia	863	2.8	6.1	11.1	6.8	4.1
Africa	893	1.5	1.5	10.7	12.5	16.2

Source: Madison, 1995.

study on the feasibility of reducing hunger by half in each of the two generations before 2050 using these variables and contrasting two different scenarios. The reference scenario projected major current trends, institutional continuity, economic globalization, and the slow convergence of developing countries toward the socioeconomic norms of developed countries. In this scenario, the number of hungry actually increased by 2050, although the proportion of hungry people declined. The "policy reform" scenario assumed that a proactive set of initiatives is instituted to achieve sustainability goals. In this scenario, hunger is cut in half with a small change in the speed of the demographic transition leading to less population, with growth in income at the higher end of plausible income growth rates, and most important, a convergence of equity to the current levels of Europe. The contrasting scenarios are shown in Figure 6-4 for the world as a whole and by region.

For these contrasting scenarios and the four major causal elements that underlie them, what are the impacts of globalization? In Table 6-3, I set out my qualitative judgments (using a scale of one plus sign [+] for small impact and four plus signs [++++] for very large impacts) as to how globalization helps or hinders the causal elements linked to chronic hunger. For *population,* globalization probably helps through a population growth rate decline by influencing all three important determinants for reducing fertility: making contraception more accessible; providing opportunities for education and work for women; and encouraging postponement of marriage through such opportunities for education and work, as well as through diffused Western lifestyle concepts.

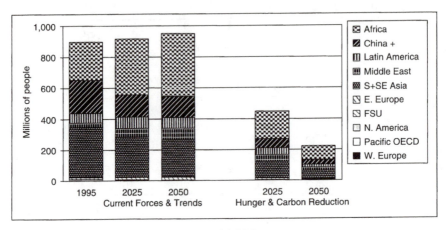

Figure 6-4. Reducing Chronic Hunger by Halves.

For *income,* globalization helps increase per capita income in some parts of the world, but practices not-so-benign neglect in others. The development of an export-oriented industry in Southeast Asia, accompanied by significant public sector actions, led to major reductions in hunger in that region until the recent financial crisis slowed and even reversed some of those gains. But in Africa, where hunger will increase most, globalization has exacerbated some of the region's problems, its export trade in such products of affluence as oil or diamonds fueling corruption and conflict, while development aid has diminished without an equivalent growth in private investment. But most of all, it has suffered not-so-benign neglect and has been marginalized from the globalized world system.

While globalization will probably decrease *inequity* overall between countries, globalization will, for some time at least, increase inequity within countries, particularly affecting the poorest of the poor. This is so because rapid export-oriented growth in developing countries reduces somewhat

Table 6-3. Globalization's Impacts on Reducing Chronic Hunger.

Causal Element	HELP	HINDER
Population Growth Decrease	++	
Increase in Income per capita	++	++ In Africa
Decrease in Inequity	+ Between Nations	+++ Within Nations
Decrease in Hunger Line		+

the differences in income with developed countries, but within countries opportunities vary greatly. Thus, for example, China, which had made enormous gains in reducing hunger, might well suffer an increase in hunger as the income gap between regions increases, as employment opportunities expand in export manufacturing and services but decline in local manufacturing and agriculture, and overall, the safety net system diminishes. Finally, the *hunger line* shifts relatively as diets expand (by preferences for both animal products and imported products or brands), more and more basic food enters the market, and the income requirement to meet these new needs increases.

GLOBALIZATION AND REDUCING EPISODIC HUNGER

Applying similar judgments to episodic hunger (Table 6-4), the reduction of famine-determined hunger from natural hazards is a great recent success story of a globalized emergency food aid system that relies on both public and private efforts. Today, famine-inspired hunger exists only where war and violent conflict persist. Globalization, however, increases famine vulnerability in the sense of entitlement shifts, as Sen (1981) has shown, especially in cases where the availability of food and purchasing power of rural landless workers can be diminished by far-off events. Globalization has increased the incidence of war and civil conflict both by making weapons easily available (the ubiquitous Kalashnikov) and by diminishing the impacts of war by providing emergency food aid. Recent financial crises often triggered by globalized movements of capital have created sudden episodic hunger in countries where such episodes were rare—as in Southeast Asia, which had made marked progress in reducing hunger prior to the crises. Finally, structural adjustment efforts initiated either internally or at the behest of the IMF almost always lead to an increase in hunger from a decrease in social services and programs, despite some counterefforts.

Table 6-4. Globalization's Impacts on Reducing Episodic Hunger.

Causal Element	HELP	HINDER
Famine	+++	+
War	+	+
Financial Crisis		+++
Structural Adjustment		++

Table 6-5. Globalization's Impacts on
Reducing Special Needs Hunger.

Hunger Type	HELP	HINDER
Mothers and Children	+++	+
Iron, Iodine, Vitamin A	+++	+

GLOBALIZATION AND REDUCING SPECIAL-NEEDS HUNGER

Concerning special needs hunger (Table 6-5), global efforts to address some major causes of child undernutrition, especially from sickness and disease, by addressing immunization, treatment of diarrhea, and breast-feeding have helped to reduce the rate of wasting and stunting of children (although the actual numbers have increased as a result of population growth centered in the youngest ages). Similarly, the major micronutrient deficiencies of iodine, vitamin A, and iron have been reduced by international programs to encourage iodizing salt, to increase intakes of vitamin A through vitamin A–rich foods and through vitamin A supplementation, and to a much lesser extent, to reduce anemia by iron supplements. In some cases the diversification of diets has helped as well—for example, by providing greater access to iodized salt. The major countercurrent related to globalization is similar to the previous case: Structural adjustment and diminished development aid have severely constrained many programs directed at addressing these special needs.

Preserving Life-Support Systems

The life-support systems of the planet are often factored into major media: atmosphere, freshwater, oceans, and the biota as biomes, ecosystems, and species. The major threats to atmosphere, freshwater, oceans, and the biota are threefold: (1) the large-scale introduction of pollutants, such as acid rain and chloroflurocarbons in the atmosphere, heavy metals in the soil, or chemicals in groundwater; (2) the massive assault on biota, such as deforestation in the tropics and the mountains, desertification in dry lands, over-fishing of marine resources, and species extinction everywhere; and (3) human-induced climate change.

These threats are incredibly recent. In nine of twelve indicators of global environmental change, half of all the change that took place over the last ten thousand years occurred in our lifetime (Table 6-6).

Table 6-6. 10,000 Years of Environmental Change: Selected Indicators.

10,000 Years of Environmental Change	Selected Indicators	
	Rate of Change Still Accelerating	*Rate of Change Now Decelerating*
Half Occurred before Our Lifetimes	Deforested area Soil area loss	Terrestrial vertebrate diversity
Half Occurred during Our Lifetimes	Carbon releases Nitrogen releases Floral diversity Sediment flows Water withdrawals	Carbon tetrachloride releases Lead releases Marine mammal diversity Sulphur releases

Source: Turner et al., 1990.

Driving Forces of Environmental Change

These changes coincide but are not necessarily caused by the most recent wave of globalization. A general consensus among scientists posits that growth in population, in affluence, and in technology are jointly major driving forces for such change and related environmental problems. This has become enshrined in a useful, albeit overly simplified, identity known as IPAT, first published in 1972 by Ehrlich and Holdren in *Environment* magazine in response to a more limited version by Commoner et al. (1971). In this identity, various forms of environmental or resource impacts (I) equals population (P) times affluence (A), usually income per capita, times the impacts per unit of income as determined by technology (T) and the institutions that use it. Academic debate has now shifted from the greater or lesser importance of each of these driving forces of environmental degradation or resource depletion, to debate about their interaction and the ultimate forces that drive them.

Let me introduce a variant of the IPAT identity (Figure 6-5)—which might be called the PC version—and restating that identity in terms of population and consumption, it would be $I = P \star C/P \star I/C$. I equals environmental degradation and/or resource depletion; P equals the number of people or households; and C equals the consumption per person of energy, materials, and information.

With such an identity as a template and with the goal of reducing environmentally degrading and resource-depleting influences, there are at least seven major directions for research and policy. To reduce the level of

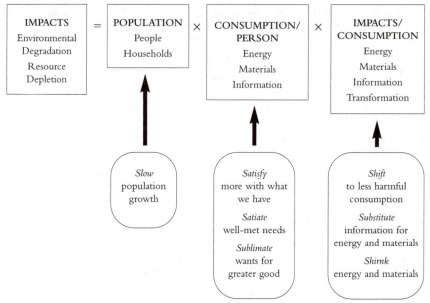

Figure 6-5. Variant of IPAT Identity.

impacts per unit of consumption, separate more damaging consumption from less harmful forms and *shift* to these, *shrink* the amounts of environmentally damaging energy and materials per unit of consumption, and *substitute* information for energy and materials. To reduce consumption per person or household, *satisfy* more with what is already had, *satiate* well-met consumption needs, and *sublimate* wants for a greater good. Finally, *slow* population growth and then stabilize population numbers as indicated earlier.

Before using these proximate determinants of the identity, a bit of caution is in order. IPAT is very useful, but is more complex than a simple identity. The PAT terms are only proximate, each in turn is driven by diverse underlying processes. Nor are the PAT terms independent of each other; for example, income (or affluence) influences the rate of population growth and consumption, as well as the technologies used to produce it. Indeed, the supposed technology term is really a catch-all of all the diverse items that determine a different set of impacts per unit of consumption—including technology, but also all kinds of ideas and institutions. Nor do I think the PAT terms are sufficient to examine the impact of globalization on Earth's life-support systems.

To add to the classic determinants, let me borrow from an analysis by Clark (2000) of environmental globalization, one that includes not only the globalization of environmental "stuff"—the energy, materials, biota transformed by production and consumption—but also the globalization of environmental ideas and governance. Specifically, Clark notes three major ideas: planetary management, risk assessment, and sustainable development; along with three forms of governance: by governments; by non-governmental organizations, both profit and nonprofit; and by coalitions and networks that bring them together.

Globalization and Preserving Life-Support Systems

Thus, there are five causal elements related to globalization's impact on preserving the life-support systems of the planet: population, consumption, technology, ideas, and governance. Examining these five causal elements (Table 6-7), beginning with *population,* globalization, as noted, will encourage a decline in the population growth rate thus lessening future human impacts on the environment. But globalization also accelerates *consumption* in three ways. Insofar as globalization increases income and to a degree inequity, it encourages greater production and consumption. Insofar as it extends the reach of trade and transport, it makes possible consumption of distant resources that would not be consumed locally and the import of goods not available locally. With the spread of ideas and images of "Western material standards of living," it further encourages consumption. Much of this enhanced consumption is desperately needed and desired by the poorer peoples of the world, but much of it will be in the form of material and energy transformations that are environmentally degrading and resource-depleting.

At the same time, globalization facilitates both the creation and the diffusion of *technologies* that lessen the need for energy and materials per unit

Table 6-7. Globalization's Impacts on Preserving Life-Support Systems.

Causal Element	HELP	HINDER
Population	++	
Consumption		++++
Technology	+++	+
Ideas	+++	++
Governance	++	++

of production or consumption, that create fewer toxics and pollutants, or that substitute information for energy and material use. Countering these helpful technologies are trickle-down technologies that export second-hand or second-rate technologies, buildings, and toxic or polluting processes to regions heretofore relatively free of degrading or depleting activities.

In the realm of *ideas,* there are also dual impacts. Development is seen as a good to be pursued, with environmental concerns a luxury that developing countries cannot readily afford. Countering this has been the rapid spread of the major environmental ideas of planetary and risk management and sustainable development, to the extent that while rhetoric persists as to differences between the North and the South, international surveys show little difference in the high environmental aspirations among the people of both North and South.

As to *governance,* while there are some 180 international environmental treaties in force to date, they are insufficient to counter the major threats to the atmosphere, oceans, and biota, with the possible exception of the Montreal protocol on ozone depletion. But as Clark notes, governance is greater than governments, and the governance activities of advocacy coalitions and the discourses between transnational corporations and international environmental groups can be very substantial in helping to maintain the planet's life-support system. Indeed, it is often the ability to draw global attention to some local threat that leads to mitigative or preventive actions. All of these forms of governance will grow with globalization. Substantially countering these forms are the notions of free trade unhindered by environmental constraint or regulation currently ensconced in the operation of the World Trade Organization and in various regional trade treaties.

Globalization and Two-Armed Scientists

The Maine version of a well-known story has Senator Edmund Muskie listening to testimony on the need for clean-air legislation. After a series of cautious scientific testimonies by scientists, he asks whether anyone in the room is a "one-armed scientist" who can testify without the endless academic qualifications of "on the one hand . . . then on the other hand . . ."

It is obvious that I must plead guilty to being a two-armed scientist. But it is difficult for anyone thoughtfully confronting globalization not to be. Indeed, whether you sing paeans to globalization as Tom Friedman

(2000) does or fear "the manic logic of global capitalism" as Bill Grieder (1997) does, the other hand, whichever it might be, is always present. What may separate the two more is that Friedman thinks that globalization itself will in time deal with its many harms, whereas Grieder believes in the need for radical revision and strong local to international action.

So, what can the two-armed scientist conclude from this first, tentative attempt to assess the impact of globalization on a sustainability transition: meeting human needs, reducing hunger and poverty, preserving the life-support systems of the planet? In this brief assessment I have focused on how globalization has affected the reduction of hunger and meeting the human needs for food and nurture and on the driving forces of global environmental change.

In sum, globalization to date has not helped reduce the numbers of chronically hungry in the world, although the proportion decreases as population grows. The shifts in investment, income, and job opportunities in some parts of the world are matched by the growth of hunger elsewhere. Episodic and special-needs hunger have benefited more as globalized public and private programs have expanded to respond rapidly to famine, to the special needs of children, and to two of the three major micronutrient diseases. Finally, the increase in hunger from globalized financial crises and policy decisions argues for new sources of instability for the fragile existence of the poorest of the poor. Short-run and long-run simulations of halving hunger argue for these trends to persist.

In preserving the life-support systems, the crucial issue is globalization's impact on current and projected production and consumption of energy and materials that are environmentally degrading and resource depleting. To date, despite major gains in technologies that reduce the use of energy and materials per unit of production, the absolute growth in consumption overwhelms the steady global technological progress. The globalization of environmental ideas has been truly remarkable, and these, along with feminism and human rights, constitute the major ideological revolutions of the contemporary period of globalization. The spread of these ideas has been well facilitated by global interconnections. Similarly, the rise of environmental governance writ large to include corporate behavior and local and international popular initiatives is facilitated by the interconnectedness of globalization and is a great portent for the future. But to date, these have all been insufficient to counter the major threats to the life-support systems, and when projected to address the extraordinary increases in the consumption of the future, such helpful developments may fail as well.

Civilizing Globalization

If the goods of globalization are to be realized for most of the world's peoples, and if its ills are to be reduced for those people and natural systems most vulnerable, then globalization itself must change in significant ways. Gerry Helleiner (2000), the Canadian economist, as well as Held et al. (1999), call this process "civilizing" globalization. All of them focus on changing governance. Helleiner asks, "Can the global economy be civilized?" "Globalized markets," he argues "operate within politically defined rules and governance institutions. The current global rules and economic governance institutions are in need of repair, updating and relegitimization," and he goes on to suggest some of those initiatives.

Held et al. (1999) focus not on economy but on politics and three major approaches to civilizing and democratizing contemporary globalization: a liberal–internationalism approach to reform global governance; a cosmopolitan, democratic approach to reconstruct global governance; and a radical republican approach to create alternative structures of governance. Exploring these issues are well beyond the scope of this chapter, but I conclude with my own thoughts on the efforts to "civilize" globalization.

Civilizing U.S. Capitalism: 100 Years

As I contemplate the varied efforts to understand globalization and how to reform or reconstruct it, I am struck by the similarity of contemporary globalization to an earlier period of American history. I perceive an analog to the current global situation in the U.S. economic history of the post–Civil War era. At that time, a truly integrated and nationalized industrial capitalism was created, spurred by the growth of interconnections of railroad and telegraph. Reading of this age of "robber-baron" capitalism, I am struck by the parallels with current globalization; for example, the great uncertainty at the time, even by the major participants, in understanding the new and different systems that had emerged.

Whatever emerged from the fierce competition and growing monopolization of economic power was initially marred by an absence of law and regulation. Much early regulatory effort was needed around what today are called "rule of law" and "transparency" issues, such as those that make contracts enforceable or stock certificates verifiable. These initial efforts were followed by numerous attempts to control monopoly power and maintain genuine competitiveness.

Almost parallel to these efforts, but much slower, were those that recognized the victims, harms, inequities, and externalities generated by the new integrated industrial system. The initial focus, as it is currently, was on child labor, followed by other working conditions, and then the essentials of a social safety net including disability insurance, unemployment insurance, pensions, and the like. Efforts to gain workers' rights began early and were repeatedly rebuffed, and it was not until 1935 that they were basically recognized. Finally, environmental issues were not really recognized until Earth Day 1970, thus capping a century of effort to civilize U.S. capitalism. Throughout this whole period the individual states of the United States served as the focus for innovative leadership and the testing ground for appropriate regulation that only later was emulated or taken over by the federal government.

The challenge for civilizing globalization is to reduce this century-long effort to, at most, two decades. The good news is that this effort is well under way, again with a push for "humanizing globalization" or "globalization from the bottom." I illustrate with Bangor, Maine, population 35,000.

Civilizing Globalization: In Bangor, Maine

Beginning in 1991, Bangor became a sister-city to Carasque, a small village in the highlands of El Salvador, as part of a group of twenty-nine such sister-cities all trying to support returned populations who had been refugees from the civil war. From Bangor, Carasque has received a rebuilt truck, pedal sewing machines, school and health materials, and, when needed, support for human and economic rights in the form of communications expressed to both the U.S. and El Salvador governments. From Carasque, Bangor has received an opportunity to learn of the realities of poor people in the developing world, a model of how young people can exercise leadership in their own communities, and instructive experience as to what alternative schooling might provide.

Trying to find an issue in common to both communities, people in Bangor identified sweatshop- or *maquiladora*-made clothes, the making of which takes jobs from Mainers and exploits Salvadorans. Today, there are a thousand consumers and thirty businesses in Bangor displaying the "clean clothes" sweatshop-free logo, and four Maine communities are now committed to selective sweatshop-free city purchasing. This has led to a statewide selective purchasing act for textiles and footwear that is now being implemented. The "clean clothes" criteria for such selective purchasing—protecting children and workers, providing a living wage, and giving workers rights to bargain—is an agenda for civilizing globalization.

Finally, many of the same Mainers recently took a five-hour trip to Quebec City, Canada, for the so-called Americas Summit to protest a free trade area until it incorporates children's, workers', and environmental concerns.

Globalization and a Transition toward Sustainability

The very notion of a transition toward sustainability, and the concept of sustainable development from which it derives, are products of the widening, deepening, and speeding up of the interconnectedness that characterizes globalization. To think of humankind as a whole, to see its links to the fate of the blue planet, has been an essential part of the globalization process. Thus, those of us who aspire to a transition toward sustainability, to meet human needs while preserving the life support of the planet, cannot be "against globalization." But what we can say (and are saying) is that for globalization to continue to encourage such a transition, it will need to redouble those aspects of this complex movement in our collective lives that help a sustainability transition and to dampen those that hinder such a transition. It is this nexus that will make real the promise of the Neem tree.

References

Anon. 2000. "Neem tree free," *The Ecologist,* 30/4:8.

Clark, William C. 2000. "Environmental globalization." In Joseph S. Nye Jr. and John D. Donahue, eds., *Governance in a Globalizing World.* Washington, D.C.: Brookings Press.

Commoner, B., M. Corr, and P. Stamler. 1971. "The Causes of Pollution," *Environment,* April, pp. 2–19.

Deininger, Klaus, and Lyn Squire. 1996. "A new data set measuring income inequality," *World Bank Economic Review* 10(3):565–591.

Ehrlich, Paul, and John Holdren. 1972. "Review of *The Closing Circle*," *Environment* 14(3):24–39.

Food and Agriculture Organization of the United Nations (FAO). 2000. *Agriculture: Towards 2015/30.* Technical Interim Report. Rome: FAO.

Friedman, Thomas L. 2000. *The Lexus and the Olive Tree.* New York: Anchor Books.

Grieder, William. 1997. *One World Ready or Not: The Manic Logic of Global Capitalism.* New York: Simon and Schuster.

Held, David, Anthony McGrew, David Goldblatt, and Jonathan Perraton. 1999. *Global Transformations: Politics, Economics, and Culture.* Stanford, Calif.: Stanford University Press.

Helleiner, Gerald K. 2000. "Markets, politics and globalization: Can the global economy be civilized?" The Tenth Raúl Prebisch Lecture, Geneva, 11 December.

InterAcademy Panel (IAP) on International Issues. 2000. *Transition to Sustainability in the 21st Century*. Conference of the World's Scientific Academies. 15–18 May 2000, Tokyo, Japan. http://interacademies.net/intracad/tokyo2000.nsf/all/home.

International Council for Science (ICSU) and the World Federation of Engineering Organizations (WFEO). 2002. *Role and Contributions of the Scientific and Technological Community (S&TC) to Sustainable Development*. World Summit on Sustainable Development. Secretary-General's Note for the Multi-Stake Holder Dialogue Segment of the Second Preparatory Committee. Addendum No. 8: Dialogue Paper by Scientific and Technological Communities. United Nations Economic and Social Council E/CN.17/2002/PC.2/6.Add.8. Advance Copy, 28 January 2002.

International Monetary Fund (IMF), Organisation for Economic Cooperation and Development (OECD), United Nations (UN), and World Bank Group (WB). 2000. *A Better World for All: Progress towards the International Development Goals*. Washington, D.C.: IMF, OECD, UN, WB.

Kates, Robert W., William C. Clark, Robert Corell, J. Michael Hall, Carlo C. Jaeger, Ian Lowe, James J. McCarthy, Hans Joachim Schellnhuber, Bert Bolin, Nancy M. Dickson, Sylvie Faucheux, Gilberto C. Gallopin, Arnulf Gruebler, Brian Huntley, Jill Jäger, Narpat S. Jodha, Roger E. Kasperson, Akin Mabogunje, Pamela Matson, Harold Mooney, Berrien Moore III, Timothy O'Riordan, and Uno Svedin. 2001. "Sustainability science." *Science* 292:641–642, April 27. http://sustainabilityscience.org/keydocs/fulltext/wssd_stc_020128.pdf.

Madison, Angus. 1995. *Monitoring the World Economy 1820–1992*. Paris: Organization for Economic Cooperation and Development.

Mathews, Jessica. 1997. "Power shift," *Foreign Affairs* 76(1):50–66.

National Research Council, Board on Science and Technology for International Development (BOSTID). 1992. *Neem: A Tree for Solving Global Problems*. Washington, D.C.: National Academy Press.

National Research Council, Board on Sustainable Development (NRC-BSD). 1999. *Our Common Journey: A Transition Toward Sustainability*. Washington, D.C.: National Academy Press.

Raskin, Paul, Gilberto Gallopin, Pablo Gutman, Alan Hammond, and Rob Swart. 1998. *Bending the Curve: Toward Global Sustainability, a Report of the Global Scenario Group*. Polestar Series, Report No. 8. Boston: Stockholm Environmental Institute.

Sen, Amartya. 1981. *Poverty and Famines: An Essay on Entitlement and Deprivation*. New York: Oxford University Press.

Turner, B. L. II, William C. Clark, Robert W. Kates, John F. Richards, Jessica T. Mathews, and William B. Meyer, eds. 1990. *The Earth as Transformed by Human Action: Global and Regional Changes in the Biosphere over the Past 300 Years*. Cambridge: Cambridge University Press.

World Commission on Environment and Development (WCED). 1987. *Our Common Future*. New York: Oxford University Press. (Bruntland Report).

Introduction

Jerry Mander makes the case against the capitalist movement that has come to be known as globalization. He reviews the globalization model, examines its focus on export-oriented production, discusses the particular depredations of globalizers against the world's forests and water supplies, and concludes that the model itself ("an idea, an ideology actually, an experiment—a guess") is inherently and fatally flawed, and that no amount of "techno-fixes" or international agreements can alter that basic fact. He also argues that the beneficiaries of globalization are, and will continue to be, those at the pinnacles of the multinational corporations, the haves, and that the have-nots and the planet itself will continue to be the victims. While Mander does not advance his own program to replace globalization, he makes clear that opposition to globalization is growing and that it has been making strides in winning "hearts and minds" and in effectively opposing multinational corporate interests.

Jerry Mander is the president of the International Forum on Globalization, an alliance of sixty organizations in twenty countries that conducts public education campaigns on global economic issues. Mander is also program director for the Foundation for Deep Ecology and is a senior fellow at Public Media Center, a nonprofit advertising company that works exclusively for environmental and social causes. In the 1960s, Mander was president of a major San Francisco advertising company before applying his talents to environmental causes. He authored several successful Sierra Club campaigns, including the one that helped prevent the building of dams in the Grand Canyon, and in 1971 he founded the country's first nonprofit advertising agency. Mander has published several books, including *In the Absence of the Sacred* (1991) and *The Case Against the Global Economy* (1996), which was awarded the American Political Science Association prize for the "best book in ecological politics."

—J.G.S.

CHAPTER 7

Intrinsic Negative Effects of Economic Globalization on the Environment

Jerry Mander

There are some intrinsic environmental problems connected to the new global economic design experiment that has come to called economic globalization. In this chapter, I begin with a broad, systemic view of the ingredients of the globalization model—its operating principles, structures, and values. Then, I focus more closely on a particular aspect, the tremendous emphasis on the rapid global conversion to export-oriented production, to show how this one aspect brings enormous, unavoidable environmental problems. I will then review some globalization issues connected to two important resources: water and forests. Finally, I briefly discuss the question, Who benefits from all this?

The reason for focusing so closely on the design model itself is that I hope to leave you with one distinct conclusion from this discussion—that many of the environmental and social problems that result from globalization are inherent in the model. If we are going to proceed with this global experiment, we are going to have some predictable outcomes, and there is no way of avoiding them. No "side agreements" or "techno-fixes" will solve these problems. They are intrinsic to the form.

We may have to change the form.

———————

I have called the globalization experiment "new," but advocates of economic globalization prefer to describe it as a long-term, inevitable process—and a done deal—the result of economic and technological forces that have simply evolved over centuries to their present form. They describe them as if they were uncontrollable, undirected forces of nature; they say that it is utopianism to believe otherwise. Of course, if we accepted this description of the inevitability of it all, as most media, governments, and universities tend to do, then obviously there would be no resistance possible and no point in talking about it. Our only option would be to lie about, watch TV, and submit, or else try somehow to take advantage of it for our own purposes. It should already be obvious that this is not acceptable to a lot of people, judging by the evidence of fifty thousand people in Seattle, hundreds of thousands in various European demonstrations, more than a million farmers in India, tens of thousands in Japan, as well as various uprisings in Brazil, Mexico, the Philippines, and even New Zealand and England. It is obvious that many people are upset at this process.

Of course, it is true enough that global trade activity and concepts such as "free trade" have indeed existed for centuries in various forms. But earlier versions were entirely different from the modern version in scale, speed, form, impact, and, most important, intent. The modern version of economic globalization definitely did not simply evolve, as in nature, like some kind of naturally dominant plant or animal species—an economic kudzu vine. Modern globalization is no accident of evolution. It was created by human beings, on purpose, and with a specific goal: to give primacy to economic—I should say, corporate—values, above all other values, and to install aggressively and codify globally those values.

In fact, the modern globalization era has a birth date and birthplace: the fateful meetings at Bretton Woods, New Hampshire, in July 1944. That was when the world's leading corporate figures, economists, politicians, and bankers got together to figure out how to mitigate the devastation of World War II. They decided that a new centralized global economic system was required to promote global economic development. This would lead away from wars, they thought, help the poor, and aid the rebuilding process.

The conferees at Bretton Woods saw themselves as do-gooders, altruists, though many had a huge financial stake in the outcome. In their wisdom, they decided the ideal instrument to keep the pieces together would be the global corporation, supported by new bureaucracies and new rules of free trade. I remember it well from my days at the Wharton School at the University of Pennsylvania and at Columbia Graduate Business School in the 1950s. I heard the global corporation loudly praised by my professors—notably, John Fayerweather and Emile Benoit—as the only instrument that could assure long-term peace, stability, and democracy. This rhetoric has not eased since. Out of the Bretton Woods meetings came the World Bank, the International Monetary Fund (IMF—with other names at that time), and then the General Agreement on Tariffs and Trade (GATT), which later gave birth to the World Trade Organization (WTO). Later clones of the model included the North American Free Trade Agreement (NAFTA), the Maastricht Agreement in Europe, the upcoming Free Trade Area of the Americas Agreement (FTAA), and quite a few others.

Together, these instruments of economic globalization have been fulfilling their mandate, which is to bring arguably the most fundamental redesign of the planet's social, economic, and political arrangements at least since the Industrial Revolution. They are engineering a power shift of stunning proportions, moving real economic and political power away from national, state, and local governments and communities, toward a new centralized model that gives great power to global corporations, banks, and the global bureaucracies they helped create, with grave consequences for national sovereignty, community control, democracy, indigenous cultures, and (more to the point today) the natural world.

The crucial point to remind ourselves about is that this process—these institutions and the rules by which they operate—have been created on purpose by human beings and corporations and economists and bankers, and have specific form designed for specific outcomes. It is no accident. It was not inevitable. And it can be reversed or revised, if with difficulty. Now, what can we say about the form?

The first tenet of economic globalization, as now designed, is to integrate and merge all economic activity of all countries on the planet within a single, homogenized model of development—a single centralized supersystem. Countries with cultures, economies, and traditions as varied as those of India, Sweden, Thailand, Kenya, Bhutan, Bolivia, Canada, Russia, and a hundred more are all meant to adopt the same tastes, values, and lifestyles; to be served by the same few global corporations, the same fast-food restaurants, hotel chains, clothing chains; to wear the same kinds of jeans and shoes; to drive similar cars; to receive the same films, television; to live in the same kind of urban landscape and engage in the same kind of agriculture and development schemes; and to carry the same personal, cultural, and spiritual values. This is global monoculture. If you have traveled a bit lately, you have surely noted the trend, entirely visible before your eyes. Every place is becoming more and more like every place else. Cultural diversity is going the way of biodiversity. Soon, there will be little reason to go anywhere at all. Such a homogenized model directly serves the efficiency needs of the largest corporations, acting on a global plain, allowing them to duplicate their production and marketing efforts on an ever-expanding terrain and to achieve the many efficiencies of scale that go with borderlessness. It is similar to the standard gauge railway of another century, or today's "computer compatibility." It is among the primary purposes of the great trade agreements and bureaucracies to make rules that assure that there are no blockages in the flow, that global corporations can move freely in all countries, and that economic homogenization and integration is accelerated.

A second tenet of the globalization design is that primary importance is given to the achievement of ever more rapid, and never ending economic growth—let's call it "hypergrowth"—fueled by the constant search for access to new resources, new and cheaper labor sources, and new markets. This is why there is such excitement about China joining trade agreements. To help achieve this hypergrowth, the emphasis is put upon the ideological heart of the model: *free trade,* accompanied by *deregulation* of corporate activity, and *privatization* and *commodification* of as many nooks and crannies of existence as possible. These even include formerly pristine elements of the global commons, elements that have until now always been far outside the trading system, areas that most of us have always assumed would remain the inalienable right of all human beings to retain in a noncommodified form. For example, there are the genetic structures of our bodies, and of all life, now very definitely being enclosed as part of the commodity trading system through biotechnology, a process hugely assisted by the WTO rules on intellectual property rights. Or consider indigenous seeds, for millennia developed and freely shared by agricultural communities for all those thousands of years, but now subject to long-term monopolization by global corporations through patenting. (Recent protests against the WTO's "TRIPS" agreement on trade-related intellectual property rights by farmers in India, and by AIDS victims in Africa and other parts of the Third World, trying to get relief from high-priced patented medicines, have begun to focus a new harsh light on some appalling aspects of this issue.) Now, we have similar pressure on freshwater—rivers, lakes, streams—probably the most basic element of sustenance, always considered to be part of the commons, available to all life, but soon to be converted into part of the global trade system. At least that will be so if the FTAA, NAFTA, and the WTO proceed with their plans. These and other resources are being rapidly privatized, enclosed, and commodified as part of the globalization project, to bring even more raw material, more territory (geographic and biological), into play for corporate access, investment, development, and trade.

At the same time, the commodification process is now taking place in the realm of public services. This is a big part of both the new FTAA agreement and the General Agreement on Trade in Services (GATS) within the WTO. Those latter negotiations concern many areas now still reserved for government, services like public broadcasting, public education, public health, water delivery and treatment, sewage and sanitation services, hospitals, welfare systems, police, fire, social security, railroads, prisons, and the like. All these may soon be commodified for the first time, privatized, and opened to foreign investment and domination. We could wind up with Mitsubishi running Social Security, Bundesbank running our jails (and maybe our parks), the British Broadcasting Corporation run by Disney; the Canadian health care system run by Merck.

In addition to all this, there is the commodification of money itself. Right now, the overwhelming majority of global transactions, under the free trade system, do not apply to goods and services, but to capital itself. Money itself is a commodity for speculation, as are financial instruments, of course. Modern information technology has made it possible to shift unimaginably large sums of money instantaneously across borders, anywhere in the world, without anyone ever observing or controlling it, by the stroke of a computer key. This has already had terrible destabilizing effects on many countries, and was surely one of the precipitating causes of the 1997–1998 financial crisis, focused in Asia. (Ironically, this free trade in money, and even free movement by corporations across borders, defies traditional free trade ideology as espoused by the late economic gurus Adam Smith and David Ricardo, the high priests of free trade utopianism. Neither Smith nor Ricardo ever believed that corporations should be mobile, or that capital should be unrooted, to leave its own community. They are surely now turning over in their graves.)

It is the job of the Bretton Woods instruments to assist this commodification, privatization, deregulation, and free trade by creating rules that require nations to conform to these principles and by trying actively to eliminate "impediments" within individual nations that might restrict corporate access to markets, labor, and resources. In practice, unfortunately, most of these so-called impediments to the system, challenged by the WTO, the IMF, and the World Bank, are laws that are legally created by governments: environmental laws, public health laws, food safety laws, laws that pertain to protecting workers' rights and opportunities, laws that try to retain controls over national culture, laws that allow nations to control who can invest on their soil, who can buy their currencies, and at what speed and under what conditions. All of these laws, even if created by democratic governments through democratic processes acting in behalf of the popular views of its citizens, are viewed by free traders as "nontariff barriers to trade" and as obstacles, subject to WTO challenges.

Though the WTO is only six years old, it already has an impressive record for challenging democratically created laws and standards. It has been particularly potent in the environmental realm. The WTO's very first ruling was against the U.S. Clean Air Act, which set high standards against polluting gasoline. The act was found noncompliant with WTO trade rules and had to be softened. The very popular Marine Mammal Protection Act—particularly the provision that protects dolphins, otherwise killed by industrial tuna fishing—was found noncompliant under a GATT rule, now within the WTO. Sea turtle protections under the Endangered Species Act were also found illegal. The United States is going back to the drawing board on these. We can expect similar challenges against U.S. or state pesticide control laws, raw log export bans, ecolabeling of products, and various "certification" schemes.

Of course, the WTO does not rule against only U.S. environmental laws. It also ruled against Japan for refusing imports of fruit products carrying dangerous invasive species. It ruled against the European Union for forbidding imports of U.S. beef injected with biotech growth hormone. This case became the basis of a threat to the European Union not to ban any biotech products, even though the European public is against biotech. In agriculture areas, the WTO has consistently ruled in favor of large machine and chemical-intensive global industrial agriculture corporations over small-scale family farming, and indigenous farmers—most appallingly in the famous Chiquita banana case. That case held that the European Union could not favor small indigenous, often organic farmers within former European colonies, over the industrial bananas from Chiquita.

The way these challenges work is truly interesting. We are led to understand that it is countries suing other countries in the WTO, when actually it is almost always countries issuing challenges to other countries' trade rules on behalf of global corporations. So the United States sues to protect Chiquita bananas, and Venezuela sues to protect its oil industry, and Mexico sues to protect its tuna industry. The net effect is that the whole process produces a mutual ratcheting downward of environmental, or labor, or health standards in all countries. It is a kind of "cross deregulation," a way that corporations can get their own governments to destroy laws in other countries, just as they pressure for deregulation domestically. The net result is that all laws and standards race downward to a low common denominator, just as is happening with global wage standards.

This is not to mention a secondary "chilling effect" from this process. For example, not long ago, the government of Guatemala cancelled a public health law that forbade baby food and infant formula companies, notably, Gerber baby food, from advertising their products as being healthier than breast milk. Canada cancelled its national ban on the gasoline additive "MMT," a well-known carcinogen. In both cases, the reasons were threats of suit under trade regimes. In the Gerber case, the United States threatened suit in the WTO. Even more remarkably, in the Canadian case, Ethyl Corporation threatened to sue Canada under an outrageous NAFTA provision, the "investor-state" provision—soon also to be in the FTAA agreement—that for the first time allows corporations to sue sovereign governments not in domestic courts but in international tribunals. The threat alleges an illegal "expropriation" by Canada, because Canada's environmental safety law prevented Ethyl from earning future profits that it might have enjoyed if there had not been a ban. A similar case has been brought against the state of California on a similar dangerous additive. California is now trying to settle out of court.

The WTO also has a similar chilling effect on Multilateral Environmental Agreements (MEAs), such as the Kyoto protocol on climate change and the Montreal agreement on ozone depletion. The WTO asserts that it has ultimate authority over these other agreements, which would mean, in effect, *corporate* authority over the environmental agreements.

There are hundreds of cases and examples. These trade bodies exist for the purpose of providing global corporations an easy way to circumvent laws that attempt to regulate them. They love to call it free trade, and what they really mean by free trade is freedom for global corporations and suppression of the freedoms for communities or nations to regulate or otherwise maintain primary values, like the environment, or health, culture, jobs, national sovereignty—even democracy.

Arguably, the most important principle of free trade is its emphasis on global conversion to export-oriented production as some kind of economic and social nirvana. This is the theory that all countries should specialize their production within commodity areas where they have a so-called "comparative advantage" over other countries in some tradable items. It could be coffee, or sugarcane, or forest products, or high-tech production (due to unusually low wages), or whatever. Each country should focus on these few areas and then try to satisfy its other needs through imports, using foreign exchange earned by exports to pay for imports. This is a crucial component of globalization theory: the idea that it is necessary to replace diverse local or regional economic systems—systems that may emphasize highly diversified, small-scale industrial, artisanal, and agriculture systems, featuring many small producers using mostly local or regional resources, local labor, and goods consumed locally or regionally. The goal is to replace these systems with large monocultural export systems.

Going back to the mid-1900s, many countries of the world had been actively trying to do the opposite, to diversify their industrial and agriculture systems precisely in order to recover from a colonial period where huge monocultural systems had been imposed on them: pineapple plantations, coffee plantations, bananas, or (more recently) industrial assembly work. Once out from under colonialism, countries saw that specialization made them extremely vulnerable to political decisions abroad or to the shocks and whims of the market and commodity pricing systems. This often left them unable to purchase basics like health products, food, energy, or basic industrial needs. Naturally enough, they sought self-sufficiency in these items. The system was sometimes called "import substitution," or simply national self-reliance. It was designed to achieve some degree of control over the overall shape of the domestic economy. Quite a few countries were doing reasonably well with this. While they were not getting rich, they certainly were getting along.

But the World Bank and the IMF applied tremendous pressures to these countries to abandon their self-reliance, which came to be synonymous with "isolationism" and "protectionism." The World Bank pressured these countries to open their borders to private investments by global corporations in a position to produce on the large scale appropriate for export. The Bretton Woods institutions made explicit threats of boycott and exclusion from the global trading system against countries that did not comply. It became impossible to get any financial aid from the World Bank and the IMF without submitting to structural adjustment schemes. Eventually, the pressure worked and effectively opened these countries to a second round of colonialism: neocolonialism.

Why were the banks pushing so hard? Here is the crux of the matter. Systems that emphasize local or regional self-reliance are extremely subversive to free trade, economic globalization, and corporate hypergrowth, which all depend upon maximizing economic processes. Local and regional production for regional consumption is the archenemy of globalization since it operates on an inherently smaller scale.

There is far less opportunity for global corporations if local populations or countries can satisfy their needs internally or regionally than if economic activity is designed to move back and forth across oceans, exporting, importing, or reworking goods, then exporting them again, with thousands of ships passing each other in the night. That's what builds global economic growth fastest, and provides opportunities for global corporate operations. But it is also what destroys the environment fastest.

A central feature of an export-oriented model is obviously that it increases transport and shipping activity. In the half century since Bretton Woods, there has been about a 25-fold increase in global transport activity. My friend and colleague David Morris, the Minneapolis economist, loves to use the example of a toothpick, which comes wrapped in plastic, and is marked, "Made in Japan." Japan is skilled in industrial production—that is one of its "comparative advantages"—but it has very few trees, and no oil. But in a global economy, it is somehow thought efficient to ship wood from some country that grows it—Chile, Canada, the United States—and also to ship some barrels of oil to Japan, then wrap the one in the other, package them in serviceable commodity units, and ship them back across oceans to consumers. That toothpick, by the time it is finally used, might have traveled 50,000 miles.

The Wuppertal Institute of Germany has made a famous study of distances that food travels from source to plate. It reports, for example, that the average components of a 150-gram strawberry yogurt travel about 2,000 kilometers (about 1,243 miles) before being combined together, and then shipped onward to consumers. The strawberries come from Poland, corn and wheat flour from Holland, jam and sugar beets and the yogurt itself from Germany, and then the plastic and paper containers and wrappings from various other places. Meanwhile, ingredients in the average plate of food on American dinner tables these days is estimated to travel on the average about 1,500 miles from source to plate. Every mile of such increased transport activity in the global economy has tremendous costs to the environment, costs that remain externalized in our current measures of efficiency, costs that eventually are subsidized by taxpayers.

As global transport increases, it requires massive increase in global infrastructure development. This is good for large corporations like Bechtel, who get to do the construction work. But it is bad news for the environments where such infrastructures are needed: new airports, new seaports, new oilfields, new pipelines for the oil, new rail lines, new high-speed highways. Many of these things are built in wilderness or forested areas with relatively intact biodiversity, coral reefs, rural areas, and the like. The impacts are especially strong now in South and Central America where there have been tremendous investments in infrastructure developments in wilderness regions, often against major resistance from native communities—particularly against oil, pipeline, and forest development from the likes of the Uwe in Colombia, the Kuna in Panama, and many different groups in Ecuador. But the problems are also obvious in the developed world. In England, for example, a few years ago, there was a mass series of protests by 200,000 people from the English countryside against the rapid development of huge new highways jammed through rural landscapes so that truck drivers could better service the global trading system. The indigenous people and the rural English are both protesting the same thing: local environment destruction from globalization.

Even more important is the increase of fossil fuel use. Ocean shipping carries nearly 80 percent of the world's international trade in goods. The fuel that is commonly used is a mixture of diesel and low-quality oil known as "Bunker C," which is particularly polluting: very high in carbon and sulfur. If not consumed by ships, it would otherwise be considered a waste product. The shipping industry is anticipating major growth over the next few years; the port of Los Angeles alone projects a 50 percent increase over the next decade.

Increased air transport is even worse than shipping. Each ton of freight moved by plane uses 49 times more energy per kilometer as when it is moved by ship. One physicist at Boeing once described the pollution from the take-off of a single 747 as like "setting the local gas station on fire and flying it over your neighborhood." A two-minute take-off of a 747 is equal to 2.4 million lawn mowers running for twenty minutes.

It is now estimated by many that the increase of global transport is one of the largest contributors to the growing crisis of climate change. If we had a U.S. government that believed climate change was real, the first thing it might do, aside from trying to meet the Kyoto standards, would be to advocate for less trade, not more. Mr. Bush is not likely to opt for that.

Increased global transport has brought other dreadful by-products. Ocean pollution has reached crisis levels, not to mention the effects of these huge ships on the ocean, wildlife, and fisheries. Even more serious, possibly, is the epidemic increase of bioinvasions, a major cause of species extinction.

With the growth of global transport, billions of creatures are on the move. They are hiding in cargo or in ballast. They are in suitcases or on our shoes or clinging to the sides of ships. From viruses to rats, from bacteria to mosquitoes to water snakes, from nematodes to exotic seeds to wild boar, from gypsy moths to zebra mussels: all are getting free transport in the global economy, and many are thriving in their new homes, often outcompeting native species and bringing pollution or health crises. Around the eastern United States, for example, the emergence of the West Nile virus where it never existed before is surely due to transport activity, as is the spread of malaria and dengue fever to other parts of North America. Even hoof-and-mouth disease is due largely to globalization.

In addition, if you are going to ship perishables across oceans, you also need increased refrigeration, with significant contributions to climate change, and an increase of packaging and of the wood pallets used for cargo loading—little noted, but significant factors in increased pressure on global forests.

So once again, the central point is this: There is no way around the problem. If you are going to design a system built on the premise that dramatically increased global trade is good, you are going to increase transport activity, and you are guaranteed to bring on the kinds of problems I have just described and many more. They are intrinsic to the model.

I want to return to the example of food and agriculture for a moment, before I move on to water and forests. It is instructive because the scale of the problem is so very great. Please remember that even in today's computer age, nearly half of the world population still lives directly on the land, growing food for their families and communities. They emphasize staples and other mixed crops. They replant with indigenous seed varieties, using crop rotation and community sharing of resources such as water, seeds, labor, and the like. Such systems have kept them going for millennia. But as I said earlier, local systems are anathema to global corporations. So companies such as Monsanto, Cargill, and Archer Daniels Midland are leading a chorus of corporate, government, and bureaucratic statements—often expressed in millions of dollars worth of advertisements—that small farmers are not "productive" or "efficient" enough to feed a hungry world. Only global corporations can do it. In the United States, we hear that, disgustingly, every night on TV on the Lehrer News Hour, on so-called "public broadcasting." Archer Daniels Midland advertises that the only thing that is preventing it from feeding a hungry world is "politics" that refuse to lower barriers for them to go in and feed everybody.

Unfortunately, such companies have plenty of entry. Nearly all the investment rules of the WTO and the big banks—and many more now proposed—strongly favor global corporations and monocultures over local diverse farming for self-sufficiency. On lands where tens of thousands of small farmers once grew food to eat, giant corporations and global development schemes are converting the land to single luxury-crop monocultures run by absentee landlords.

These companies absolutely do not grow food for local people to eat. Global corporations favor high-priced, high-margin luxury items—flowers, potted plants, beef, shrimp, cotton, coffee—grown for export to the already overfed countries. As for the people who used to live on the lands, growing their own foods, they are rapidly being removed from their lands, and they are not getting jobs, either. Since these corporate systems feature highly intensive, machine and pesticide production, there are very few jobs. So the people who used to feed themselves become landless, cashless, homeless, dependent, and hungry. Communities that were once self-sustaining disappear, and still-intact cultures are decimated. This is even so in the United States, where there are now very few family farmers left.

Eventually, the farmers and their families flee to crowded urban slums. There, without community, without cultural supports, they try to compete for the rare, poorly paid, urban job. Families that once fed themselves become society's burden, while huge corporate farmers get rich from exports.

Some of these newly landless peoples also start fleeing across borders. We have certainly seen that in the context of U.S.–Mexico trade, since NAFTA. For Mexico's indigenous Mayan corn farmers, who supported themselves via the *ejido* co-op farming system in Mexico for nearly a century since the Zapatista revolution in the early 1900s, NAFTA has been a death sentence. In order to qualify for NAFTA, Mexico had to kill off the *ejido* system, opening up the Mayan farmlands to entry by outside investors, driving the Mayans off their lands. Landless, homeless, cashless, these people have often fled across the U.S. border looking for seasonal work as grape or strawberry pickers, only to be met with xenophobia and violence.

The environmental problems that are intrinsic to this shift to export are immense. Monocultural production, virtually by definition, drastically reduces biodiversity, not only by killing the microscopic life within the soils through heavy chemical use, but also by reducing production of commodities to one or two export varieties. Where indigenous Filipinos, for example, once grew thousands of varieties of rice, now two varieties account for 98 percent of production, and the other varieties are disappearing. Mexico has lost more than 75 percent of its indigenous maize varieties. Among potato farmers on Chiloé Island in Chile (as well as in other parts of the Pacific slope of the Andes where thousands of varieties of potatoes were once grown) production has been reduced to four or five varieties suitable to large-scale intensive production. According to the Food and Agriculture Organization (FAO) of the United Nations, the world has already lost up to 75 percent of its crop diversity.

Consider also the external costs of industrial agriculture. Hailed as more efficient than small-scale farming, it is a kind of efficiency that ignores the costs of air, water, and soil pollution. It ignores the toxic rivers and the dead fish, as well as the loss of topsoil from heavy pesticide and machine-intensive production. In addition, the increase in the use of fossil fuels and in public health problems from foodborne diseases is directly rooted in factory-farming systems. *Salmonella, E. coli,* and *Listeria,* as well as mad-cow disease, hoof-and-mouth disease, and others are consequences.

Finally, there are the social costs of somehow taking care of all the farmers who have lost their livelihoods through this system, which brings social and environmental costs into the billions of dollars. Most of these problems are direct results of the switch to industrial agriculture production designed largely for the export trade. Taking all these external costs into account, is it not preposterous to call this system efficient? Maybe one can get a tomato from Mexico for a few cents less at the local store, but all pay more in higher taxes in future years to clean up the messes this system causes. But it is the environment that pays the most.

Now, the companies offer biotech as a "clean" solution. But, let us ask this: When corporations patent indigenous varieties of seeds that communities of farmers have developed for millennia, and then genetically alter seeds so the seeds will not reproduce—these are so-called "terminator" seeds, thus assuring that farmers must buy new seeds annually from the corporations—does anyone really believe this has something to do with feeding the hungry? Obviously, it is not the goal of corporate agriculture to feed the world. That's just their advertising slogan. Their goal is to feed and further enrich themselves.

Millions of farmers around the world are exquisitely aware of the global corporate agriculture system, and they hate it. It is fair to say that farmers have been the leaders of international resistance to globalization in many parts of the world. We have seen mass protests by rice farmers in Japan, Thailand, and the Philippines. We have seen gigantic protests against Cargill, Kentucky Fried Chicken, and Monsanto in India, with millions of people on the street. Two years ago, we saw a French farmer named Jose Bové drive his tractor into a McDonald's in France. Bové was protesting "bad food," he said, as well as the entire industrial agriculture system, the corporate takeover of small farmers, and the destruction of traditional farming in France; the cultural and ecological destruction that goes with undermining the artisanal small-scale cheese and other production in

France; and the harsh rules of the WTO's *codex alimentarius*. Among other rules, *codex* recently stated that cheese could no longer be sold in outdoor markets in France, unless it was shrink-wrapped, just like Kraft's.

Once again, we must note that it is the economic model itself that is the problem. The whole idea of converting diverse local economies into gung ho export trade systems can only benefit global corporations while making individuals, communities, and nations dependent and vulnerable. Society, communities, and the environment would be far better off if international institutions and agreements put maximum emphasis on aiding local and national self-sufficiency, rather than maximum exports.

There are two other trade-related resource issues that need to be mentioned: water and forests. Both are now hotly prized commodities, and are the targets of new initiatives in the global trading system.

As many people already know, there is a looming crisis in the global freshwater supply. Freshwater represents only one-half of 1 percent of water on the earth, and the amount is not increasing. Meanwhile consumption of freshwater is doubling every twenty years. Population growth is not the problem. The rate of increase in water use is twice the rate of population growth. Why? Human beings use only about 15 percent of the global freshwater supply. Sixty-five percent goes to industrial agriculture (which uses it at a much higher rate than do small farmers) and to high-tech production, especially for computer chip manufacture, which requires absolutely pure water. High-tech production is increasingly moving to low-wage Asian countries such as China, whose own water supply is already nearly used up. Meanwhile, the United Nations reports that now more than 1 billion people on Earth lack access to clean drinking water.

The matter is beginning to be so serious that it is bringing quite a few nations to the brink of war. It is one reason, for example, that Turkey is at war with its Kurdish population, which seeks independence: The Kurds live in the mountain region that supplies Turkey with its water. It is also an issue among quite a few African nations, between Israel and its neighbors, and even among the United States, Mexico, and Canada.

As the water crisis gets worse, one would expect governments and global bureaucracies to advocate conservation. Instead, what is being proposed, as usual, is to privatize, commodify, and globalize the planet's remaining freshwater—its lakes, rivers, streams—to sell exploitation rights to corporations, and let the global market decide who gets to drink it or use it. NAFTA and the WTO already have provisions that define water as a "commodity" and "a tradable good"—no longer protected as part of the commons—and they have rules requiring that governments permit foreign investment in local freshwater supplies and exportation of the water under certain trigger conditions. One such condition is that if any locality anywhere in the country—a city or a province—privatizes any part of its freshwater resources or delivery operations and opens it to bidding by foreign investors, then the entire country is obliged to follow suit, and it may not ever reverse the decision. In other words, if British Columbia proceeds with its plans to allow a foreign investor to run its water delivery system, then all of Canada's lakes and rivers are open to exploitation and export forever. It sounds like some sort of absurd joke, but it is deadly serious.

Of course, corporations are totally excited by this. Water, after all, may soon be arguably more valuable than oil. Among the brilliant new corporate schemes to exploit this situation is one that ships North American lake, river, and stream water across to Asia, where the need for it is growing due to industrialization of agriculture and investment by high-tech industries. Picture this: Supergigantic supertankers, bigger than any current oil tankers, filled with freshwater, steaming across oceans while also towing humongous floating plastic balloons the size of a baseball park, carrying a big part of Lake Superior to China, to Bill Gates's operation there.

Just as with the agriculture industry, which likes to say it is feeding a hungry world, the new emerging water industry likes to say it is bringing water to a thirsty world. But not only will most of the water go to industrial users, once water systems are fully privatized and globalized—a process that is being massively aided by the new GATS agreement, as well as the FTAA—most of the people on the planet who are actually thirsty will not be able to pay for it. Who will get the scarce water? Bill Gates or the peasants in Bolivia? The answer is obvious. Actually, a preview of what is coming recently happened in Bolivia, where a water privatization scheme by the government—giving Bechtel corporation the rights to own and sell the local water supply and sharply increase its costs to customers—was met with demonstrations by tens of thousands of poor and indigenous people who finally got the government to back off and Bechtel to withdraw. This is only the first of many such confrontations we will see in Bolivia and elsewhere.

Now, let us look at forests. One of the victories of the protest movement in Seattle was that it succeeded in focusing some attention—some of it led by my colleague Victor Menotti—on the WTO's proposed "advanced tariff liberalization initiative," also known as the "free logging agreement." This was strongly backed by the United States. It would have eliminated tariffs on all wood products. Industry predictions have been that by eliminating all trade barriers, global consumption of paper products alone would increase by 3 to 4 percent. That would be very beneficial to the giant forest-product companies of the world, but devastating news for the world's forests, particularly the frontier tropical forests, where much of the planet's remaining biodiversity is located.

I would not be surprised if some environmental sciences scholars are inclined to favor this initiative. Nonetheless, I must report some alarming aspects. Even without the free logging agreement, the situation in the world's forests is desperate. The world's biodiversity is becoming extinct at very high rates. Some authorities predict that as much as two-thirds of all plant and animal species, mostly in the tropics, will be completely lost by the second half of the twenty-first century. The world's primary forests are among the last remaining large reservoirs of biodiversity—particularly the tropical forests in such places as Brazil, Mexico, Indonesia, and Cameroon, and the temperate forests in Canada, Russia, and Chile.

But forestry corporations are already successfully pressuring governments about three basic elements of public policy relating to forests. All of them are at various stages of being introduced into the WTO and other trade agreements:

1. *Unregulated access to the world's remaining forests.* As supplies of forests in the United States dwindle, U.S. producers need to get at the forests of Mexico, Brazil, Indonesia, and the like. But to do that will require changes of domestic law in those countries and/or changes in the rules of the WTO and other international agreements so such countries are required to allow greater investment and access, and fewer environmental controls. Once again, it is cross deregulation. That is the assigned role of the WTO and the free logging agreement.

2. *Increased access to consumers.* The targets here are domestic tariffs on wood and wood products, local building codes that may require non-wood construction materials, any distribution systems that may favor domestic companies over foreign investors, and any other environmental initiatives such as ecolabeling or certification, which global forestry corporations are hoping to outlaw via a WTO rule.

3. *Minimized regulatory costs.* Companies want to get rid of national, state, or provincial environmental laws that, for example, prohibit cutting on steep slopes, or in habitats of endangered species or are too close to rivers, and so on. Corporations strongly prefer operating in countries where such environmental laws are poorly enforced or nonexistent. The industry wants the WTO to impose standards that are universally low.

One top industry executive told the U.S. International Trade Commission that the U.S. Endangered Species Act "is the largest single burden on the competitiveness of American forest products . . . it has got to go," and the U.S. forestry industry is eager to install new WTO disciplines that will uniformly restrict governments from any regulation of destructive logging practices. The American Forest and Paper Association is now actively lobbying to impose its own regulatory standards, called the "sustainable forestry initiative," as the standard to be followed by the WTO. This is an outcome that would make standards of forest protection as weak as the current standards for food protection in the *codex alimentarius.*

In any case, as with all the other examples, the point remains the same: The free trade system is there to help global corporations overcome and control regulations that might inhibit their pursuit of resources and markets, whether it is water or wood or agricultural land. The Bretton Woods system is an instrument of corporate purpose. That is its job.

I could address further toxic dumping, large dams, power grids, depletion of fisheries, and effects on indigenous peoples around the world, all accelerated by the development schemes of the IMF, the World Bank, and the trade and development model they both promote. All of it occurred because of an idea, an ideology actually, an experiment—a guess—that this model of economic development is good, and that it will have long-term benefits sufficient to justify all this destruction.

One could grant the benefit of the doubt to the architects of this global experiment. Let us say they meant well. Maybe they really believed that this system would produce a kind of rapid exponential growth that would be truly beneficial. We have certainly heard them repeat the main homily over and over: "A rising tide will lift all boats," the claim that its benefits would trickle down to all segments of society, that the real purpose is to help lift the poor. But is that true?

How could anyone really buy this? First of all, how can hyperexpansion be sustained? How long can it go on before we have to directly face the limits of a finite planet? Where will the resources—the minerals, the wood, the water, the power—come from to feed an exponential expansion, without killing the planet? How many cars and refrigerators can be built and bought? How many roads can cover the landscape? How many fish can be industrially vacuumed from the sea before the ecosystem fails and the species disappear? How much pollution can we live with? How much global warming before the social and environmental costs become too great?

Anyway, who finally benefits? It is not the farmers driven from their lands and made into homeless refugees. It is not urban dwellers, dealing with influxes of displaced peoples, jamming in looking for jobs. It is not workers caught in downward wage spirals, and it is surely not nature.

It is obvious who benefits. Here in the United States, we know that top corporate executives of the largest global companies are making salaries and options in the millions of dollars, often in the hundreds of millions, while real wages of ordinary workers have been declining. The Institute for Policy Studies reports that American CEOs are now paid, on average, 450 times more than production workers, with that rate increasing yearly. The Economic Policy Institute's 1999 report says that median hourly wages are actually down by 10 percent in real wages, over the last twenty-five years. The *New York Times* reported that even as the U.S. economy has begun to slide, executive salaries of large corporations, mostly global corporations, are steadily increasing, into the upper hundreds of millions. In the computer industry, which led our recent boom, where some people have famously made fortunes, 80 percent of assembly and production workers are temporary workers: $8 an hour, no benefits, no unions. Are we lifting all boats yet?

The U.N. Development Programme's 1999 *Human Development Report* indicated that the gap between the wealthy and the poor within and among countries of the world is getting steadily larger, and in part it blamed inherent inequities in the global trade system. Such is the degree of wealth concentration from all this that the world's 475 billionaires are now worth the combined incomes of the bottom 50 percent of humanity.

Of the largest one hundred economies in the world, fifty-two are now corporations. Mitsubishi is the twenty-second largest economy in the world. General Motors is twenty-sixth. Ford is thirty-first. All are larger than Denmark, Thailand, Turkey, South Africa, Saudi Arabia, Norway, Finland, Malaysia, Chile, New Zealand, and so on.

If you still cling to the nostalgic idea that big corporations are helping employ the global workforces—that size begets jobs—here is one final statistic: The two hundred largest corporations in the world now account for about 30 percent of global economic activity, but employ less than one-half of 1 percent of the global workforce. As these companies continue to get larger and more globalized, they continue to replace workers with machines or buy up competitors and eliminate duplicate jobs. Such economies of scale are intrinsic to the free trade, globalization design, just as environmental pollution is intrinsic to export-oriented trade. Large-scale mergers and consolidations—bigness—produces fewer jobs, not more jobs.

So much for the rising tide that lifts all boats. Clearly, it lifts only yachts.

That is the bad news. The good news is that it does not need to be this way. There is nothing inevitable about the present system. It is just a set of rules and institutions that we can change if we want to. If we have a democracy (do we?) then we can change it. A lot of people understand this, and are mobilizing to change it, as we have seen in Seattle and other places. As for the WTO, it was so worried about anyone wanting to monitor its October 2001 meeting that it moved it to Qatar. The WTO has clearly not learned much yet about openness, transparency, and democracy, for Qatar is a great place to hide.

Nonetheless, tens of thousands—hundreds of thousands—of opponents of globalization are moving forward. Most are in general agreement that the Bretton Woods model is hopelessly flawed, as it responds only to one set of values: that what is good for corporate growth is good for all of us, and for the environment, too. It is already clear that does not hold up.

There is now also major grumbling inside the WTO. Schisms have developed on such issues as biotech, agriculture, services, and culture. Some countries are feeling great heat from their citizens about destruction of traditional livelihoods, the health risks of the agriculture trade system, or the pressures that the United States applies for massive conversion to industrial corporate agriculture models.

In Seattle, we saw for the first time that Third World countries have understood that the present system is not designed to help them, despite the phony WTO rhetoric. They understand increasingly that it is designed to exclude them, or to keep them as resource and labor colonies for global corporations.

A great illustration of this happened during the protest in Washington, D.C., in April 2000, against the IMF and the World Bank. The banks were giving daily briefings to the press blaming the protestors for harming the world's poor. It was the same thing that Michael Moore, president of the WTO, had been saying in Seattle, claiming that the WTO was the one working for the poor and that environmental activists were harming them. The *New York Times* and *Washington Post* and all the networks dutifully carried surely one of the most cynical statements in history: the claim that environmentalists were harming the poor. But then one day I picked up a copy of the *International Herald Tribune*. It had a front-page story about the IMF charges that environmentalists were harming the poor, but right next to it, with equal space, the *Herald Tribune* carried a story about the G77 meeting in Havana, which was going on simultaneously with the WTO meeting in Washington, D.C. In Havana, the world's poorest and least developed countries had voted unanimously to praise the protestors and sharply criticize the IMF and World Bank.

That story was not carried in the *Post* or the *Times,* though it did appear in Europe and Asia. We have quite a bit of work to do with the media, including getting them to carry some stories about why people protest rather than focusing only on fifteen to twenty anarchists.

But the best news, I think, is that most of the opposition no longer feels we should let the people who created this problem also provide the solution. Two years ago, some twenty-five thousand of these people—from all parts of the world—gathered in Brazil to begin a global process of moving toward a replacement for the Bretton Woods model. The hope is to define a new set of international agreements that operate from an entirely different, noncorporate hierarchy of values. Of course, one did not read much about this meeting in the media either, because the media was all in Davos, Porto Alegre, where the captains of industry and globalization were meeting at the same time at the so-called World Economic Forum.

Our own organization, the International Forum on Globalization, is very involved in this process of defining alternative recommendations and engineering an international consultation process to develop and refine them. We have been on this track since before Seattle, actually with many people in the leadership of the movement—notably, Martin Khor of the Third World Network; Vandana Shiva (see Chapter 9); Lori Wallach from Public Citizen; John Cavanagh from the Institute for Policy Studies; David Korten; Maude Barlow of the Council of Canadians; Walden Bello of Focus on the Global South—among twenty others.

In conclusion, let me ask that everyone keep in mind that there is nothing inevitable about globalization. It is a designed system, an experiment, a set of rules made by the people who most benefit from them. We showed in Seattle that we do not accept them, and we will keep saying that. As for the charge that we are the utopians, obviously they have got things backward. If there is utopianism, then it is corporate utopianism that is the problem. To keep arguing that a system that homogenizes global economic activity and culture to benefit corporations, that removes power from communities and puts it into global bureaucracies, that marginalizes and makes homeless millions of farmers and workers, and that devastates nature in entirely unprecedented ways can survive for long is corporate utopianism. I do not think it is going to work.

References

Mander, J. 1991. *In the Absence of the Sacred: The Failure of Technology and the Survival of the Indian Nations.* San Francisco: Sierra Club Books.

Mander, J., and Goldsmith, E. (eds.). 1996. *The Case Against the Global Economy.* San Francisco: Sierra Club Books.

U.N. Development Programme. 1999. *Human Development Report 1999.* New York: Oxford University Press.

Introduction

Stephan Schmidheiny looks at globalization's specific effects on forestry and the wood products industry from a business perspective. He calls upon his diverse experience as an international investor and executive and condenses his observations of the global forestry market into eight major trends. His insightful discussion touches on such topics as forest certification, genetically modified trees, the increase in plantation forestry in the Southern Hemisphere, and investments in sound forestry practices. Schmidheiny also emphasizes the importance of building partnerships between the business and academic communities, two sectors that he believes could mutually benefit from cooperative interaction. His analysis, overall, encompasses a number of very real threats to this volatile industry and to the planet, but it is fundamentally an optimistic view of the future. Having invested in and developed business concerns founded on the idea that a sustainable forestry industry can indeed profit and flourish in a global marketplace, Schmidheiny offers us a practical and immediate vision of the amelioration of a global industry whose health is so directly tied to that of our biosphere.

Stephan Schmidheiny is an international business leader. He is also founder and president of AVINA, a foundation encouraging leadership for sustainable development in Latin America, and of FUNDES, a concern that promotes small business enterprises in Latin America. He owns Grupo NUEVA, a business with interests including pine plantations, forestry products, pipe systems, construction materials, and specialty crop agriculture. In 1990, he was named as the principal business adviser to the secretary-general of the Rio Earth Summit, Maurice Strong. He then founded the Business Council for Sustainable Development (now the World Business Council for Sustainable Development). In addition to his many interests and business activities, Schmidheiny is also the author of *Changing Course: A Global Perspective on Development and the Environment* (1992) and *Financing Change: Eco-efficiency, Sustainable Development, and the Financial Community* (1996).

—J.G.S.

CHAPTER 8

Forests and Globalization:
A Business Perspective

Stephan Schmidheiny

In 1982, at a time when everyone who had a chance took their money out of Chile to escape a pending devaluation, I decided to take part of my own patrimony out of my Swiss bank account and to invest in a forestry venture in Chile.

I spent almost a month touring the country's back roads chasing more than a dozen investment leads. The choice was not easy; everything was for sale—cheap—except the one company that I liked best because it was small and well-managed by a private entrepreneur. He would not even receive me to talk about selling, but I managed to convince him to consider a partnership, whereby I would bring in new equity in exchange for a 50 percent share. The company, then, owned some 10,000 acres of pine forest and a sawmill tiny by today's standards. Half of the trees harvested were exported as raw logs; the most elaborate product back then was rough-sawn green lumber.

Today, eighteen years later, I own 85 percent of Terranova, a Chile-based company with plantation forestry operations in that country, Brazil, and Venezuela. Another of my companies has teak plantations in Panama and Guatemala. Terranova owns 296,000 acres of forests in Chile, 20,000 acres of forests in Brazil, and 280,000 acres of forests in Venezuela. The great majority of this acreage is pine plantations, although the Chile holdings contain more than 80,000 acres of native forests, which are managed for conservation. The Panama and Guatemala holdings include teak plantations and natural forests. Terranova produces doors, moldings, doorskins, and fiberboard, most of which is exported to the U.S. market. We no longer sell logs, but products with added high local value.

The growth and performance of my investment in the Latin American forestry industry looks meager compared to recent dot.com paper value explosions. But it does look quite decent compared to high performers in what is today referred to as the "old economy," of which my company forms part. So it is with an underlying feeling of achievement and pride that I share my investor's experiences in forestry.

All of our forests are recent plantations, mostly planted on degraded farmland. The Chilean company is quoted on the Santiago stock exchange, and is accredited under ISO 14,000, an accreditation I and my colleagues at the World Business Council for Sustainable Development helped to develop back in the early 1990s when we were looking for practical ways to make that somewhat foggy vision of sustainable development operational in business terms.

Earlier this year, we were wondering whether to seek accreditation under the Forestry Stewardship Council (FSC). In preparations for the certifications process, we ran into an unexpected challenge: The FSC requires cooperation with indigenous people, and anyone else, living in one's forests. My own "forests" are small, scattered plantations, and almost by definition, no one lives in privately owned plantations. Thus, FSC accreditation did not seem appropriate for us. But while we dithered, Home Depot—which sells a substantial amount of our products in the U.S. market—said we had to prove our forestry operations were sustainable. So we are now busy seeking FSC accreditation. The Panama plantation gained FSC certification in August 2000.

I could almost stop this chapter right here. I, a Swiss entrepreneur, need approval by a nongovernmental organization (NGO) based in Oaxaca, Mexico—namely, FSC—before I can export wood products produced by a Chilean company from plantations in Chile to the nine hundred stores (stretching from Canada to Chile) of an Atlanta-based multinational. This is the reality of doing forestry business in the present global market. Further, it is a reality that is only a few years old.

The Business of Forestry: Eight Major Trends

What is going on in this ever volatile sector, the business of forestry? Writing this chapter forced me to assess my own experience and to consult others. I condensed the results into eight major trends. The news is not all good, but there is more good than bad.

In offering these trends, I would like to contribute to a dialogue through which we in business and those in academia can develop ways to make the most of some trends and resist others.

First, despite present chaos and controversy, I think we are moving toward standardization of international environmental–management norms. At present, there are many different standards and certification schemes—far too many. Environmental groups hate this lack of coordination, as it results in confusion for the customer and threatens the value of all standards. But it is even more annoying—not to mention expensive—for business. We must look far into the future and make long-term management decisions based on expected market demands. Yet, with many standards and rapidly shifting market expectations, it is very difficult to plan over the long term. For this reason, I think that in five to ten years, it is probable that there will be one or a few generally accepted standards that will characterize good management.

We currently see steps in this direction. For example, the FSC is developing regional standards that will meet local requirements, but will all fall within a framework of "global principles." Also, there are efforts toward a pan-European framework for mutual recognition of national certification schemes within Europe, and perhaps even other regions.

We who grow trees in developing countries will have to meet those standards to sell in industrial countries. Thus, we should also be involved in deriving them. Indeed, the World Business Council has a task force of forestry companies defining their own concept of sustainable forestry and promoting the need for mutual recognition and standardization of forestry certification systems.

The second trend: We are going to see much more labeling, backing up consumers' rights to choose. We have already seen the development of a significant market for forest products coming from well-managed forests. Labeling and chain-of-custody procedures allow customers to identify such products. Proof that forest products come from well-managed forests is likely to become the cost of entry to most or all developed country markets; this is already the case in much of Europe and is increasingly the practice in North America. Having borne that cost, I am a bit disappointed that proof of state-of-the-art management is not reflected in a significant price premium for such products. Consumers do not feel that they should pay more for such a product. I hope they will at least buy it in preference to uncertified products.

Speaking of labeling, one big unknown now is the market acceptance of forest products from genetically modified (GM) trees. It is likely, based on experience in Europe with agricultural products, that consumers will demand genetically modified organism (GMO) labels. But this is impossible to predict. Will consumers accept GM forest products because—in contrast to their appetite for GMO potatoes—they do not eat trees? Or will they be impressed with the possibility of producing trees with less lignin, so less energy and chemicals are required to extract the cellulose— a great environmental benefit? Or will they be horrified that GMO trees stay in the environment for many more years than do GMO soybeans? No one knows.

Labeling does offer some opportunities to us business people. We can differentiate our products on the market. There are also dangers: If a forestry company invested heavily in GM trees, for example, and there is little market acceptance down the road, its products could be identified and avoided.

A third trend—one of which my own company is a typical example— is a general forest business shift to the tropics and the Southern Hemisphere. Growing conditions are better there, and labor, land, and materials tend to be more cost-effective. These last considerations are important for me, as I am trying to add value—turn trees into doors, for example—in the countries where we grow the trees. (I am not in the pulp business.)

However, there are business challenges to operating in developing countries, such as political and economic instability, high-risk premiums on the cost of capital, corruption, and logistical difficulties. Also, since some types of forestry are relatively new, the techniques may not be well known in the tropics. These risks have diminished in much of Latin America over the past decade, but they have not disappeared.

Such challenges are particularly important because of the long time frame inherent in forestry investments. Nevertheless, these problems can be overcome, and we will see an increasing plantation forest estate in the tropics. High international environmental standards and market expectations encourage companies operating in and exporting from the tropics to employ the latest in global technology and management practices. Some of the most modern and professional forestry companies are located in tropical developing countries. Being involved in plantations rather than natural forests also cuts risks in that intensive plantation forestry requires a much smaller land base, which can be privately owned, thus reducing a company's exposure to the risk that a government will change the terms of a forestry concession.

This leads to my fourth trend: a general move away from logging in primary forests, and perhaps even native forests altogether. The public in industrial countries is gradually concluding that the logging of primary forests, tropical or temperate, is not a legitimate use for these forests. They feel that these forests have been diminished to such an extent that most should be conserved. Right now there are large protests in the Elaho Valley of British Columbia, and there are numerous municipal boycotts in Europe and the United States, where communities have banned the use of tropical woods over the past decade.

This is not to say that there are not opportunities for an investor to manage native forests for timber, but any such efforts will be held to extremely high standards. Indeed, it was concern over tropical deforestation that originally led to the creation of the Forest Stewardship Council. Even investing in an FSC-certified forestry company operating in primary forests seems pretty risky to me. Many of the NGOs feel strongly that in some of the more endangered forests there should be no forest management permitted at all, even if it is of the highest standard.

There is another important aspect to this trend. Based on past rates of plantation establishment, there may be an abundance of plantation wood on the world market by as early as 2010. This will make it very difficult for operations in tropical native forests to compete, particularly in basic products such as construction timber, woodchips for pulp, or plywood. If steps are not taken now to develop new markets and management systems that can produce higher value products in these forests, then operations in native forests in the tropics are likely to face severe price pressure. This will make it much more difficult to manage these forests responsibly. Thus, sheer economics are likely to reinforce the growing public sentiment that natural forests should not be managed for timber.

A fifth trend is the growing specialization of forests for different products and services. For forests and plantations that produce timber, we see a reduction in the number of species planted, and a reduction of the within-species genetic diversity of the trees that are planted. Furthermore, genetic engineering now raises possibilities of tailoring the genetic codes of trees to produce specific products. For example, there are lines of *radiata* pine with reduced lignin content for pulp, and different lines of trees with reduced branching for industrial timber. There is even talk of developing carbon forests—plantations of trees that have been bred to absorb the most carbon dioxide possible.

This trend for increasing specialization is a natural outcome of companies focusing on specific markets and competing to reduce the costs of their production. However, it contrasts strongly with the scientific and NGO view that forest managers should manage for all of the wide range of goods and services that forests produce; management must not be limited to a narrow band. There is also less tolerance for logging or other extractive uses in conservation forests. It is fair to say that conservationists are also demanding their own specialty forests.

How do we resolve the two trends—the increasing demand that forests be managed for multiple goods and services, and the increasing specialization at the stand level? I think it is by increasing the scale at which we consider forestry issues. We need good regional or landscape-level planning that designates forests dedicated to conservation and designates areas of intensive production. However, such planning is missing from much of the world, particularly in the tropics. In the absence of such a plan, forestry investors will find that they will be expected to provide the full range of goods and services from their managed forests, an expectation that plantation foresters will find quite a challenge to meet.

In my own forests, in the absence of regional land-use planning, we try to adopt a systemic approach, but on a smaller scale. Rather than try to manage a large area of native vegetation for many different purposes, and risk not achieving any of them, we have areas of forest of intensive production, areas for watershed protection, and areas for conservation.

Based on my own experience, I think that the industry should take the lead in pushing for regional forest plans and for the establishment of protected areas. This is in our own self-interest, as it will help companies to engage in a constructive dialogue about what we can and should accomplish on our own lands.

My sixth trend is the increasing scale of operations and more use of economy of scale. Many forestry companies, in both developed and developing countries, are relatively small—too small to be listed on stock exchanges. They do not have access to international capital markets, nor can they afford the best genetic material, top-notch technical staff, and knowledge. Their unit costs are also considerably higher than those of a larger forestry company. These conditions have led to a trend toward globalization of forestry companies. As companies increase in size through mergers and acquisitions, they can meet listing criteria for stock exchanges and thus gain access to capital markets. They also achieve economies of scale and become more competitive.

Nevertheless, small forestry companies will always play an important role in many countries and markets. We need to find ways to support the needs of small-scale producers. One way to overcome the financing problems of small, individual companies is to group small companies within a larger forestry fund. These funds assume ownership of many smaller forestry companies, and become large enough to secure state-of-the art professional management, to gain access to capital markets, and to offer investors the chance to invest.

In Central America, we are experimenting with ways of overcoming other disadvantages that small-scale producers face. My foundation, AVINA, is funding an initiative called Teak 2000, a program in which my companies are actively participating. The goal of Teak 2000 is to group small-scale producers together so that they can gain access to technical knowledge, market knowledge, and genetic material. We are at the beginning of the experiment; we do not know if this will work. The major question is whether business people will be willing and able to cooperate together for their own mutual benefit.

Another example of this experimental mode is the development of new partnerships with the academic community. Our companies in Panama and Guatemala are too small to support their own research and development programs. Yet, because there is little experience managing teak in a professional manner in the region, there is a great need for new knowledge. We have thus established a mechanism for cooperation between the public research institutes and the private sector. We have a scientific steering committee that meets twice a year and identifies the most pressing problems relating to the sustainability of the plantation operations. We then host graduate students to work on these issues; two masters students from Yale University were working on our lands this year. As far as we can see, this is a win-win situation for all concerned: We get access to top researchers; Latin American students have the opportunity to conduct research on real problems facing the forestry industry; and the research institutes have the opportunity to demonstrate that they are working on and contributing to issues facing their region.

One bit of bad news—my seventh trend—is that no serious market for environmental forest services seems about to emerge, despite a lot of talk about the high values of these services. There are still no significant markets for biodiversity, watershed protection, or carbon sequestration. Until markets emerge for these services, there is no financial incentive for forestry owners to manage for them. But there are public expectations that they do so, and investors are being asked to manage for these services. Such services would add to the costs of timber production but bring in no additional revenue. This must change. The need to provide incentives and compensation to forestry companies is increasingly recognized. For example, Forest Trends, the new Washington-based forestry NGO, has chosen this theme to be one of its major campaigns.

I want to end on a trend of particular interest to those involved in the study and implementation of forest policy: Governments are playing a decreasing role in forestry management. This is something I called for in my 1992 book, *Changing Course,* noting that over the past few decades some three-quarters of the world's forests had been brought into government ownership. I also noted that this government stewardship had not been a great success.

Today, the major forest dialogues are between industry and the NGO community. They are bypassing government. Government is still in the business of leasing out the forests, but has less influence on what happens in them. There must be more effective partnerships among business, academic and research institutes, and NGOs. Most recent developments in forestry—such as standards, emerging markets for green products, demand for consumer labeling, shift of responsible forestry companies away from logging of primary forests—have all taken place without the significant involvement of government.

NGOs are working to offer the public more and better information on forestry issues. Business people must therefore expect that information on our operations and forests will be posted on Web sites hosted by such organizations as Global Forests Watch, World Conservation Monitoring Center, and Forests Monitor. This information will greatly increase the ability of civil society and consumers to engage the forestry sector in dialogue. Thus, it is in businesses' interests to form direct dialogues with NGOs, consumer groups, and other citizen groups interested in constructive dialogue, as these are stakeholders that will determine market access and demand for forest products. These market trends are happening outside the sphere of government regulation.

There are several ways that the forestry industry can accelerate the multistakeholder dialogue that is now beginning to take place. Business must be more willing to discuss—and be more honest about—the impact of the forestry sector as a whole. The leading companies need to "name and shame" the poor performers in their industry, who bring the entire sector into disrepute. The industry also needs to be more honest about the impact that poor and irresponsible logging practices have on forests around the world and work on ways this can be mitigated. We should put our full support behind the establishment and maintenance of protected areas throughout the world's forests. Finally, the forestry sector also needs to be more willing to enter the public debate. Responsible forestry companies employing best practices are some of the best stewards of the land. They have a right, and a responsibility, to become involved in the evolving dialogue over the fate of the world's forests.

For their part, NGOs and academics must study and understand the current realities of the forestry business, so that they can play a helpful role in moves toward solutions. They must recognize that demanding too much of forestry companies will put them out of business, unable to compete against much less benign uses of land such as agriculture.

These steps taken by those interested and involved in the forestry industry would greatly facilitate the dialogues that must take place in order for the world community to arrive at a plan for the world's forests that meets everyone's needs. One of these discussions is actually called "The Forest Dialog"—co-chaired by the World Business Council for Sustainable Development Forestry Working Group and the World Resources Institute. It is a small panel of fifteen members, drawn from the private sector, private landowners, and the NGO community, that will spawn the creation of working groups on key forestry issues, such as certification, illegal logging, sequestration, and GMOs. There is a lot of goodwill among members of this group, as there is not a lot that separates progressive industry from NGOs that are open to engage business in a constructive dialogue. The challenge is reforming the poor performers in industry, and in keeping fringe NGOs from counterproductive actions.

There is only one certainty as to the future of the forestry sector: We shall see change at a much faster pace and with far more dramatic consequences than this industry has seen in the past. Even though trees are a symbol of steadfastness and forestry is seen by some as a kind of epitome of the "old economy," this sector will see sweeping changes.

We in the forestry business need the help of global forestry and environmental studies schools to change in ways that sustain the world's forests and their myriad services—and in ways that sustain our businesses. Let us in business and academia join forces to see to it that we move as far as possible toward that illusive goal that ought to inform all of our activities: sustainability.

References

Schmidheiny, Stephan. 1992. *Changing Course.* Cambridge, Mass.: MIT Press.
Schmidheiny, Stephan. 1996. *Financing Change.* Cambridge, Mass.: MIT Press.

Introduction

Vandana Shiva reviews a period in which the debate on globalization seemed to shift, a year when she believes key propositions of globalization were exposed as myths or falsehood, and large-scale grassroots protests captured the world's attention. The chapter touches on many themes: "undemocratic" treaties, unsustainable development, global trade's destruction of local markets, trade-related intellectual property rights, the spread of genetically modified crops, and the struggle to prevent the rollback of many early successes in environmental laws and practices. Her prime concern is people—those whose lives and livelihoods she sees as damaged or destroyed by the march of globalization. Shiva propounds the need for new democratic governance based on local communities and empowered people. Her work in India in the Jaya-Panchayat ("living democracy") movement has given her hope that where national governments and international organizations have largely failed to protect the environment and the least powerful in society, smaller, local groups can achieve success through a more direct form of self-rule and the more profound community of all living things on Earth.

Vandana Shiva holds a Ph.D. in theoretical physics and is the founding director of the Research Foundation for Science, Technology, and Ecology in India. Author of *Violence of the Green Revolution, Ecology and Politics of Survival, Monocultures of the Mind,* and *Biopiracy,* in 1993 she was awarded the prestigious Right Livelihood Award, known as "the alternative Nobel Prize," which recognizes path-breaking work in environmental issues that apply a "human touch" to the application of science in environmentally friendly ways. She also directs a seed conservation project and is part of the Indian National Environmental Council. Her work has brought her international acclaim, and she spends much of her time lecturing around the world on issues concerning the environment, development, and globalization.

—J.G.S.

CHAPTER 9

The Myths of Globalization Exposed: Advancing toward Living Democracy

Vandana Shiva

There were many myths about globalization at the beginning of the 1990s, but the 2000–2001 period saw many of those myths exploded. The most important casualty was that globalization is an inevitable force of nature and that all we can do is adjust to it. Until 1999, the messages coming from U.S. President Bill Clinton and U.K. Prime Minister Tony Blair amounted to "adjust, adjust, adjust, adjust."

The proponents of globalization have had as their dominant idea the notion that once we have global market integration, everyone will have more goods, everyone will consume goods without limits, and everyone will be happy. Out of this vision of a globally integrated market came the fantasy that, somehow, poverty will get alleviated. The globalists' mechanism of choice for this is the "trickle-down theory"—a rising economic tide lifting all boats—despite the fact that the past twenty years have raised very serious questions about whether the trickle-down theory works at all. Yet trickle-down theory has remained a touchstone of the free trade theorists—their magical recipe for poverty reduction. Their assumption remains that people and nature need to adjust to the rules of trade, trade being the beginning and end of their vision of globalization.

Globalization proponents cling also to a self-serving theory of how environmental protection arises. To summarize this view, the poor are hungry and will destroy the environment; only rich people will protect the environment; when everyone's rich, the environment will prosper. Therefore, let us make everyone rich, and of course globalization is the path to riches. Globalization will bring about universal wealth, environmental safety, peace, and democracy.

Every one of these myths had to be given up recently. That is the

141

message from Seattle, from Davos, and other sites of anti-globalization protests. It is now acknowledged that globalization is not a force of nature; it was and is a plan of the powerful. It devolved into very concrete rules, created out of very specific meetings, in which particular kinds of actors had more decision-making power than others.

It was therefore not an accident that, along with the protest in the streets, it was the African countries that put their foot down at the World Trade Organization (WTO) ministerial meeting in Seattle. These nations refused to continue to act as rubber stamps for committee statements written and negotiated without their input; they refused to sign agreements that did not recognize their needs. I believe that the African countries finally realized that they had nothing to lose and needed to take strong action. India, my country, used to be a very strong negotiator at the intergovernmental level. In fact, throughout the Uruguay Round of General Agreement of Trade and Tariffs (GATT), it was India that raised questions about new issues such as intellectual property, agriculture, services, and investment being brought into a trade treaty. Sadly, in more recent days, India's government seems so interested in the short-term benefits of having a few software export licenses and a few more software engineers that it is willing to trade away benefits and principles crucial to our farmers, their livelihoods, and the environment.

The G-7 countries have played a major role in the consolidation of power, to which I have referred, and so have, behind the scenes, the major corporations. For example, after the negotiation of the WTO Agreement on Trade-Related Aspects of Intellectual Property Rights (TRIPS) during the Uruguay Round, a representative of Monsanto actually went on record at a meeting in Washington saying that for this treaty, Monsanto did something unprecedented: it wrote a treaty, took it to the U.S. government, then took it to the GATT secretary as the draft of the new property laws—governing the world of agriculture, medicine, entertainment, everything. The executive concluded, "And we were the patient, the diagnostician and the physician all in one."

Of course, when that starts to happen, you have a total convergence of unaccountable power. In the last ten years, I have witnessed the fact that global marketing configurations have led to market closure and exclusion for local producers, placing the power to control the markets firmly in the grasp of large, industrialized, nonresident producers. So, necessarily, when people leave because they cannot continue in their traditional livelihoods because their local markets have disappeared, poverty is being created, not reduced. Global marketing has also led in general to more ecological destruction, because globalized production processes tend to be far more resource demanding. They have high external environmental costs that are usually not considered by the trade agreements that advance them, and they thus effectively overrule the democratic power of people to prevent environmental destruction.

As millions lose their livelihoods, millions lose their democratic rights. But eventually, as we have seen, they will stand up to protest, as is their democratic right. Of course, when the people protest, there is likely to be more governmental, military, police, and corporate repression, which will often be used by the beneficiaries of globalization to paint those who oppose globalization as criminals, agitators, anarchists, and the like. Those who seek to control the protest of people who are being oppressed by globalization are trying to make it appear that such protest is the cause of a cycle of violence and unrest growing in society. In this way, they can try to identify anti-globalization efforts not with increased peace and democracy, but with more conflicts, more polarization, and more exclusion.

What has happened in the past year is that nearly everyone from the trade and economic community who used to treat globalization as an unstoppable force is now advocating its adjustment. The "party line" is no longer that globalization will automatically produce prosperity; now, it is that we have to adjust globalization for sustainability, we have to adjust it for equality. It is quite doubtful, however, that the same people who have created the rigid rules that prevented globalization from being a more flexible, adjustable process are suddenly going to be able turn all that around.

As an example of the kinds of basic changes that must occur if we are to have any meaningful adjustment of the process, we can look to a phrase that has appeared in many trade treaties, such as the North American Trade Treaty, the GATT Uruguay Round, those of the WTO: "a barrier to trade." Workers' rights have been considered as barriers to trade. Environmental protections have been treated as barriers to trade. Requirements guaranteeing people's basic needs are considered barriers to trade. I think the transition to sustainability—the "adjustment"—requires that we start thinking in terms of barriers to sustainability and barriers to social justice, because unless we find a way to grapple with those barriers, we will not be able to make the transition.

We must also recognize how these pro-globalization treaties work in practical terms. The GATT treaty, for example, started as four hundred pages of rules and thousands of pages of data, and this data keeps piling up. In fact, most governments have stopped keeping many of their figures covering what is happening in terms of the environmental and social impact of globalization. Instead, they are all delivering data on the aggregate measure of support and tariff structures of many thousands of commodities. They are, in fact, generating data for continued negotiations, though there is no agreement requiring them to do this. The result is that globalization's impacts on the natural world and local cultures are ignored in favor of the impacts on economic goods and services. The well-being of humans and other living things is traded for the well-being of commodities.

There are effects of the treaties that are outside the treaties themselves. By equipping parties to the treaties with the power of cross-connected trade sanctions through the trade rules, a member nation can force any country—even nonsignatories—to adhere to trade rules. But the more serious issue is that the black-and-white rules do not stay on paper: The rules turn into political processes in society as governments, institutions, and corporations align themselves to the trade requirements, which in turn empowers certain elements of society and disempowers others. As a result, the rules start to change our institutions, and that is what people experience.

Quite clearly, none of this process is written in the treaty rules, but it is that process that destroys jobs, destroys ecosystems, and creates dictatorial, authoritarian tendencies in our societies. The time has now come to see what these treaties are doing to real people and real ecosystems, and to correct both the rules and the unwritten rules that have come out of them. That is the first step in the transition to sustainability.

We must understand that globalization has not really been about increasing global communication between markets and peoples, but about creating an environment of deregulated commerce at the global level. But deregulated commerce at the global level required two things simultaneously: the deregulation of environmental protection and the over-regulation of commerce at the local level. The last ten years of my work have chiefly been concerned with resisting the dismantling of every environmental achievement of the 1970s and 1980s. Deregulated commerce at the global level required over-regulated commerce at the local level. This is a consequence that most people cannot see from a distance; they experience it only when a law applies to them in their own community. These overly heavy local rules come in all kinds of garb. For example, they may come in the guise of health or hygiene standards. One reason that U.S. farming has increasingly shifted into factory farming and created more food system hazards is the pseudo-hygiene laws that replace actual health measures with requirements for equipment and gadgets. Recently, under a new international hygiene standard, Brazilian poultry farmers were told they could not export eggs unless they had stainless steel equipment. Can you imagine in these little shantytowns that farmers are being told to buy stainless steel washbasins and other very expensive apparatus?

In a case I am dealing with right now in India, an announcement came to all small-scale industry, all street vendors, and all cycles and rickshaws in Delhi, the capital: "Beware, if you don't have a license." Normally, in the pre-globalization era, if I was at home, I could just walk outside and there would be a woman making hot, fresh tea at any time you wanted it. She is now illegal. Of course, you cannot dispense overnight with something traditional like that in a city of 20 million people. So, what happens is that most such illegal small business people started to bribe policemen in order to get by. Obviously, this contributes to corruption and disrespect for the rule of law. Hygiene does not come from gadgets, but from access to clean water and functioning municipal services, which the privatization so often brought through globalization takes away from the poor.

I want to share with you some of the major issues that have kept me very busy over the past decade—issues all related to biodiversity, sustainable uses, sustainable agriculture, and sustainable fisheries.

In the case of agriculture, we were repeatedly told by organizations such as the International Monetary Fund (IMF) and the World Bank that Third World countries should not grow staple crops. They did not have competitive advantage, and the comparative advantage of feeding themselves should wait upon the development of a new market for farmers from the Midwest of the United States. In the meantime, Third World nations should grow flowers and shrimp and vegetables. If you look at any trade agreement-based structural adjustment prescription for any Third World country in the last decade, that is what it is supposed to do.

Basic or subsistence foods are, in general, low-valued goods. Shrimp and flowers are high-value commodities, so you can supposedly sell them on the export markets, and make a lot of money, with which your country can buy food, and so have growth. Unfortunately, it does not work that way, because when every country starts to grow shrimp, shrimp become cheap. When you import products such as rice and meat, they keep rising in cost. In India, we have had a fourfold rise in food prices in recent years, this in a country where 300 million are already hungry, where 90 percent of the income of the poor was for buying food. If they were already spending 90 percent buying food and were half-fed, when the food is four times more costly, you can imagine what they are doing—eating less. That is where malnutrition comes from. That is where disease of the poor comes from. Interestingly, shrimp farming can be done in temperate zones. This industry has been moved to the Third World by the global food corporations partly because of the environmental costs, which are heavy and take many forms. In trying to recreate the sea on land, using huge pumps to bring seawater onto fields, there is the danger of seepage: The salt water seeps into the local groundwater, and soon the area has no drinking water. I came to know about this issue because the women in the coastal areas of India started to destroy the shrimp farm ponds in protest, and when they were arrested, they wrote to me and said, "We've done this, we think it is an environmental problem, we need an environmental study, come and help us." So I came to investigate and saw major environmental disaster areas: coconut trees dying and paddy fields wiped out because of salinization caused by globalized food production businesses that were supposed to be more productive than the crops they replaced.

Swedish environmentalists have done a tremendous job of assessing these shrimp farms and their environmental footprints. These studies, and ours in India, have examined the destruction of agriculture, water, and mangroves. Only 13 percent of the feed given to a shrimp converts into protein. The rest goes to waste and becomes pollution, which is then pumped out daily into the sea and, of course, is degrading sea fisheries. So more fishermen lose their occupations. Fisheries, land-based agriculture, and forests are all damaged or lost. For every dollar traded globally by exporting shrimp, between seven to ten dollars is destroyed locally in resources. Shrimp farming also requires that you catch 15 times more fish at sea than the weight of shrimp that will be produced: the sea fish are used to make the food fed to the farmed shrimp. Thus a "sustainable" industry requires even more unsustainable sea fishing. There are many such shadow costs to globalized industries.

There are also very similar figures for meat exports—a factor-of-10 destruction (spending at least 10 times the amount of resources to produce and transport one unit of meat)—a figure that never gets discussed or negotiated in the WTO because individual countries do not keep those records.

The Danish Environmental Ministry did a fascinating study some years ago that showed that 1 kilogram of food traded globally generates 10 kilograms of carbon dioxide. Thus, imports that replace local crops have the shadow cost of increased carbon emissions (and also bring with them many other forms of pollution). Two examples of this type of ill-conceived global "swapping" will suffice. Recently, England exported 111 million liters of milk and imported 173 million liters. It imported 49 million kilograms of butter and exported 47 million. In India, in 1996, the World Bank told the government that storing grain was bad, whereas shipping was good; storing was inefficient, shipping was wonderful. So in that year, India exported 22 million tons of wheat, which was sold in India at $60/ton and which sold for $240/ton internationally, in June. But then we did not have surplus wheat in December and ran short. Thus, in December we imported wheat, now at $240/ton. India lost on foreign exchange, and the poor had to pay for wheat many times the cost. In addition to that, if 2 million tons had just stayed at home, it would not have generated 20 million tons of CO_2. The Gujarat earthquake of January 2001 followed the Orissa cyclone of 2000, a storm of about 300 kilometers per hour. India never had cyclones of that kind of speed before. We did a study and found that it was approximately 50 percent higher in speed than past cyclones (there were other cyclones in the Bay of Bengal, but not at that speed). Because the shrimp farms had destroyed the coastal mangroves, there was no natural buffer. As a result, the Orissa cyclone had a serious impact, and communities that had never been affected in the past did not know how to deal with it. Thirty thousand people died, along with about 100,000 cattle. To the degree that global climate events may be linked to the environmental destruction brought about by globalization—and I believe that this link will be increasingly well demonstrated—we will see a vicious cycle: more globalized trade leading to more global environmental destruction that will require more global trade, and so on.

The government of India is now proposing a superhighway around the coast. We already have a highway and a train track. The new superhighway's only advantage would be that it is even closer to the sea and therefore it would supposedly save a few cents per ton in the transport of goods. We must ask, however, what happens when you have a highway wall 40 feet high hit by a cyclone driving a tidal wave 50 feet high: All that salt water sits on the inland side of the road and cannot drain out. We have already had examples of seawater rendering agricultural land infertile in this way; a new superhighway, combined with continuing climate change, is a recipe for further disasters.

Globalization has definitely meant the globalization of nonsustainable industrial agriculture, such as higher use of pesticides and more expensive seeds, which means debt, unpayable debt, in the context of national poverty. In India, the land of karma, where we always believed that things got sorted out in the next *janam* (rebirth), for the first time people realize that we have to sort it out *today* with the moneylender. And who is the moneylender? The agent of the same global company that sells the pesticide and the seed. So, in India we see multinational corporations serving as moneylender and seed/pesticide agent in one, withdrawing traditional low-interest credit—another destructive element of globalization. These private moneylenders/sales agents charge for credit at 30 percent to 100 percent—usurious rates. This is absolutely outrageous. Over the last two or three years, my colleagues and I have been analyzing the number of people in Indian villages who have committed suicide. We document more than twenty thousand peasants who have been driven to suicide due to high costs of seeds and pesticides in a deregulated market for agricultural inputs.

Since 1995, the benchmark date of intensive globalization, in two regions particularly—Andhra Pradesh and Punjab—we have seen a 6,000 percent increase in pesticide use. Warangal, which is in the state of Andhra Pradesh, used to grow multiple food crops, and there was no chemical agriculture. It has had a 2,000 percent increase in pesticide use, leading, I believe, to suicides and new poverty. People take desperate measures to survive. We are finding fast-rising cases of kidney sales. A moneylender will say to a debt-ridden farmer: "Okay, I'll arrange for the sale of your kidney, you'll be fine, makes no difference." And the poor man submits to the surgery. Some men permanently lose the ability to work. Their wives and children must go to work, and all are condemned to a life without education, without savings, without hope of improvement.

There is a wonderful cartoon about Andhra Pradesh, which is also an electronics state. India has a cyber chief minister, Chief Minister Naidu, who promotes electronic commerce and information technology. The cartoon shows him sitting with his laptop outside his office. There is a farmer saying, "You do e-commerce and I do me-commerce. I sell my kidneys as a result of your policies." These are among the day-to-day preoccupations in our country.

Let us consider the introduction of genetically modified crops in India. Monsanto held a press conference in 1998 to say they had brought them to India and next year would be selling them commercially. Our seed laws held that a company needed to test new crops for two years, and in the case of genetic engineering, to follow the laws and rules for import and export, storage of hazardous microorganisms, and genetically modified organisms (GMOs). All of these laws were in place by 1989, but Monsanto did not think it had to bother about them at all, just about the trials. My group found out where the trials were being held and learned that many of them were being invalidated. We took the case to the Indian Supreme Court based on violations of environmental laws related to import and deliberate release of GMOs under the 1986 Environmental Protection Act. Unfortunately, this case is going to be difficult in part because of a great deal of tainted research intended to support the case for GMOs. The case is still pending in the Supreme Court.

India used to have a National Patent Law that tried to create a balance between promoting production and innovation and taking care of people's access to medicine, food, seeds and agricultural inputs. Among the core areas of our law was a "no patent" clause for agriculture and life-forms. We have now lost this protection under the new TRIPS agreement. This overly broad agreement allows companies to patent life-forms, seed, and virtually all the intellectual property knowledge that society has.

I call this biopiracy, one of the greatest excesses of globalization. In 1994, the W. R. Grace Company took out a patent on the Neem tree for use as a pesticide. Neem, *Azadirichta indica,* has been used for millennia in our indigenous health care and agriculture systems for medicine and pesticide (see Robert Kates's Chapter 6, "The Nexus and the Neem Tree"). My group was startled to find sixty-four patents on Neem products. We challenged one and won the case in May 2000. Even though the European Patent Office told us we would get the written judgment in six weeks, I am still waiting for it.

Another major case of biopiracy is that of basmati, which is a traditional aromatic rice from India. A Texas-based company called RiceTec started to market a series of traditional rices; they call one "Texmati American-style Basmati." In addition to all the labels for trademark, the company has a patent that claims it created a novel rice, despite the fact that identical strains have been grown in India for centuries. My group spent a lot of time challenging them, and RiceTec has withdrawn three claims, but not the seed and the plant claim. However, in August 2000, under pressure from citizen's groups, the U.S Patent Office struck down 90 percent of the claims of RiceTec. We have a long legal and political fight ahead of us to win the rest of the battle against this indefensible patenting of this most basic and traditional staple.

Beyond matters of intellectual property, let us consider what globalization does in regard to market access for traditional, local products. Over the last five years, imports of agricultural products have gone up from 50,000 million rupees in 1995 to 200,000 million rupees (approximately US \$40 billion), a 400 percent increase. India used to be the biggest producer of edible oils in the world. It had the most amazing biodiversity—sesame, coconut, peanut—many of them evolved in India. In 1997, we imported 236,000 tons of soya oil. In 1999, it had shot up to 800,000 tons because India is not allowed to have restrictions on any crops as a result of a U.S. dispute with India and a WTO rule. What has this meant? The prices of other edible oils have started to collapse. Mustard, a favorite oil in India, has gone down in price from 2,000 rupees a quintal to 900 rupees a quintal.

Coconut in one year has gone down from 10 rupees a head of coconut to two. The state name Kerala is derived from *kera,* which is coconut. In the land of coconut, people are now talking about cutting down coconut trees and coconut gardens, which means Kerala will not be Kerala anymore. Sixty-five percent of coconut cultivation has disappeared, and more than 600,000 (60 percent) of India's small virgin oil extractors, who used to produce the best oil, have shut down. It is now illegal in India to sell open oil—oil not sold in closed bottles or cans—which means it is illegal to sell fresh oil produced the traditional way. So, if the only legal thing for a billion Indians is to consume as many aluminum oil cans and plastic oil bottles as those in the West, an enormous amount of new environmental harm is on the way.

The lesson from these examples is that if we can retain and improve local food systems, we can increase democratic control over food quality and reduce or eliminate expensive and wasteful packaging and processing. But this is not what is being dictated by new global trade agreements in the name of open market access and integration.

In the same category, we must look at what happens in a country like India when quantitative restrictions on imports are removed, prices of a staple food are fixed between a few monopolistic suppliers, and subsidies from the richest nations destroy the "level playing field" that is the supposed goal of the WTO. I have documented such a case in regard to soya, which, because of the biased market produced by removed import restrictions, price fixing, and unfair subsidies, has become a major threat to India's biodiversity and its farmers' livelihoods. Once again, there are other shadow costs, the externalities of environmental destruction that are never counted in the production costs.

I want to stress that none of this can happen without real violence against people. The violence is related to the fact that the people whose livelihoods are affected protest. Just last year I had to go to rallies in Sira, where two farmers were killed, as well as in Multai where fifteen farmers were killed. In protests against the aquaculture movement, six people were shot dead in various parts of India by the police. These numbers may seem small on their face, but they indicate a much larger population driven to the edge by undemocratic changes imposed on them from without and an increasing level of state-sanctioned repression in response to legitimate protest. In 1993, before the conclusion of the Uruguay Round, we saw a protest of half a million farmers in Bangalore, basically telling the Indian government not to sign the treaty because it would destroy our agriculture, upon which 75 percent of Indians depend. Those protests have continued. Almost every day there is a protest somewhere in India, and some are dealt with violently by corporate security forces and the police. Protests are growing, and people are finding new ways to protest. I believe that protest is the first step in resistance but that the second and bigger step is building concrete alternatives institutionally in both production systems and consumption systems.

In this context, how do we make the transition to sustainability?

We are in an unstable situation in which three upside-down pyramids—our global economic system, our global political system, and our global environmental systems—have the least powerful in their shadows. The economic pyramid assigns high value to markets, but little or none to local economies. Regarding the environmental pyramid, most natural resources should remain unexploited, to maintain nature's vital processes; instead, most natural resources are being sucked into global markets. Little is being left for the sustenance of the people, and next to nothing is being left for nature's maintenance. In politics, democracy requires that people be empowered locally because that is where they can truly act and influence, and through local action address national issues. People want secure ways to influence their representatives. Since most people live and work at local levels, that is where the democracy should be the strongest. A few of us—the CEOs of global corporations, some governments, and a few troublemakers (like myself)—manage to reach the global domain, but that domain will always remain a remote area of influence for the majority of people of the world. So what should be a tip of the political pyramid is now at the base, a far-reaching erosion of democratic power at the national and local levels.

These three upside-down pyramids need to be put back in order because they are thoroughly unstable, ready to fall at any time. Our current global systems are explosive—economically, environmentally, and politically.

We first have to start removing the political barriers to transition. We need to bring a balance between commerce, ecology, and social and political equity. That is why we have started the living democracy move-ment, to re-localize political power and economic activity.

For me, the use of the term "sustainability" is very clear. It is the main-tenance of the ecosystem over time so that our rivers are not dead, our lakes are not polluted, our species are not extinct. It is also social sustain-ability: Peoples must be able to maintain their cultures and diversity, main-tain their livelihoods, and maintain their economic security.

Sustainability means something very different to large multinational corporations. A paper on Monsanto's water policy that was leaked to me will serve as an example. Basically, the first five pages talked about the global agrarian water crisis, how little freshwater is left in the world, how much pollution exists, and how water diseases are spreading. The paper went on to say that this will make a perfect market, a growing market, and that the sustainability of this market should be on the company's sustain-ability agenda. For many corporate interests, sustainability means the sus-tainability of the return on investment, and very often all other concerns and definitions are lost. Such businesses ignore nature's economy and the people's economy. The only economy they consider is that of the company, and it must continually be growing.

That is why we have to bring nature and people into the picture. Sus-tainable water use means leaving enough water for ecosystems and the sur-vival needs of the people. Sustainable food systems means leaving enough food for species survival, for local consumption, and for national food secu-rity. This approach implies organic agriculture and local food systems with global trade only in genuine surpluses. Our living democracy movement, based on the people's sovereignty, strives to achieve balances in food, water, and biodiversity democratically, through just and sustainable use of resources.

We need to continue the work of international environmental gover-nance. But we still also need to do the work of stopping the reversal of environmental gains to allow people and resources to sustain themselves into the future. The environmental problem can only be solved through a commercial system that creates positive linkages with the environment. What we need are strategies for creating environmental democracies, an Earth democracy, in which all species have rights and human action is based on full awareness and recognition of rights of all people and all species.

Living democracy has a true respect for life, for equitable sharing of the earth's resources with all those who live on the planet. Living democracy has a strong and continual articulation of such democratic principles in everyday life and activity, not just once in four or five years, because that is not good enough. Living democracies must ensure that democratic institutions are decentralized, rather than being centralized, unaccountable systems of power.

The way we have started in India is through a movement we called the "Jaya-Panchayat," which means, literally, "living democracy." It is spreading like wildfire. We started it in twenty villages. We have reached four thousand villages in a year, and they are shaping their own systems of what they call free colonies, freedom zones. We will not accept dangerous chemicals, we will not have GMOs, we will not have patents on life, we seek to resurrect sustainable systems that we had, and we will learn to advance new, sustainable technologies.

The success in India that we have had with the Panchayat grows out of three things. First, we have a constitutional amendment recognizing decentralized democracy as the highest form of democracy, one where the local village community or town community has more powers than the parliamentarians regarding major areas of law, especially natural resources use, development planning, and the like. It is an example of true self-rule; the people in these communities are saying, "We rule in our village and we will negotiate with government about what powers we want to delegate to them." The national government makes decisions on the basis of the principle of subsidiarity already enshrined in our constitution. And global investments and trade have to respect local democracy. This goal was achieved successfully in the case of Dupont in Goa, where the local community refused to allow Dupont to set up a nylon plant. It was subverted in the case of Enron in Maharasthra, and now the Enron power project has failed and is up for sale. Local communities can create better checks on how money is spent and what development projects are really doing. Direct democracy also does a better job of rooting out corruption, as the Right to Information movement in India has shown.

Second, the Panchayati-Raj is an elected body, and a panchayat by law has to have 30 percent women. This is therefore a more inclusive, less sexist, more balanced form of governance.

The third thing that we are doing is that we are widening that concept to converge with the deep consciousness that we call "Vasudhaiv Kutumbkam," the earth community. This is not just the panchayat in the formal sense but the panchayat in the ecological sense of community, of all lives that must work together. The building of these new freedom zones, which ensure the protection of all species as well as the livelihoods of the poor, is creating a new potential and challenging the idea that you need to destroy the planet before you can save it. A new vision of a globalized world can come out of this potential: a globalization based not on free trade (that is not free) or open markets (which are not open), but on the true community of living things on a living planet.

References

Jafri, Afsar. *Removal of Quantitative Restriction.*
Lucas, Caroline. 2001. *The Great Food Swap: The Greens in European Parliament.*
Shiva, V. 1998. *Mustard or Soya.* Navdanya.
Shiva, V. 2001. *Starving People, Rotting Grain.* New Delhi: RFSTE.
Shiva, V. 2002. *Yoked to Death.* New Delhi: RFSTE.
Shiva, V. 1997. *Biopiracy: The Plunder of Nature and Knowledge.* Boston: South End Press.
Shiva, V., et al. 1997. *The Ecological Costs of Globalisation.* New Delhi: RFSTE.
Shiva, V., et al. 2000. *License to Kill.* New Delhi: RFSTE.
Shiva, V., and Ashok Emani. 2001. *The Orissa Super Cyclone.* New Delhi: RFSTE.

CHAPTER 10

Environment and Globalization after Johannesburg

James Gustave Speth

"Obviously, this is not Rio," said U.N. Secretary-General Kofi Annan at the conclusion of the World Summit for Sustainable Development (WSSD) in Johannesburg, South Africa, in September 2002. Indeed, it was not. The Earth Summit ten years earlier in Rio de Janeiro was a landmark event. It produced an outstanding blueprint for sustainable development, *Agenda 21*; two major international conventions on climate and biodiversity protection and a commitment to a third on desertification; Forest Principles for sustainable forest management; the beginnings of the Earth Charter; the important Rio Principles to guide international decision making; and a commitment to double development assistance funding. By contrast, WSSD's Plan of Implementation was a faint echo, though it contained a few notable accomplishments.

Whether you judge the Johannesburg Summit a failure or a very modest success depends on the measuring stick you apply. If you ask whether the summit responded seriously to global-scale environmental threats, or brought globalization and sustainable development together, the only honest answer is that it did not. In failing to rise to the moment, WSSD was a huge missed opportunity. Environmental leaders were almost unanimous in voicing dismay, though they did not lose their sense of humor. The World Wildlife Fund called WSSD the "World Summit on Shameful Deals," and Greenpeace noted that the Plan of Action on energy "is not much of a plan and contains almost no action."

When the heads of state took the podium in the final days, speaker after speaker attacked the plan as too weak, and after formally agreeing to the text, the delegates from almost two hundred nations applauded for just ten seconds. U.S. Secretary of State Colin Powell was heckled. The anger at the

United States was palpable. Not only was President George W. Bush not among the 104 heads of state in attendance, but the United States had fought with considerable success against tough targets and timetables, including the European proposal to set a goal of having 15 percent of countries' energy provided by renewable sources by 2015. Iran, Iraq, most of the OPEC countries, and Japan joined the United States in this successful opposition.

Almost everyone in the preparation for Johannesburg accepted the proposition that the excellent agreements reached at Rio had not been effectively implemented and that this failure had been compounded by declining, rather than increasing, development assistance. WSSD, therefore, was to be about implementation. The Natural Resources Defense Council said WSSD should be the "Down to Earth Summit."

A year before the summit, Maurice Strong, who ably led the previous environment and development conferences at Stockholm and Rio, wrote that "what is needed for Johannesburg is a clearly stated theme or goal, together with concrete measures and firm commitments to specific targets designed to measure progress along the way." I was among those who firmly agreed with Strong that Johannesburg would succeed if agreements were reached on specific plans of action to which governments were unambiguously committed, with targets and timetables and commitments to funding. Nothing else could close the huge credibility and accountability gaps that had opened since Rio.

I had been scheduled to discuss these matters with Secretary-General Annan on September 11, 2001, and I arrived at Grand Central Station just as the first of the twin towers collapsed. When I did finally meet with the secretary-general in October, we went over possible areas where concrete plans of action with specific, funded, and time-bound objectives might be framed for WSSD. These areas included (1) providing secure, committed funding and other support needed to meet the Millennium Development Goals, including the goal of halving world poverty by 2015; (2) complementing the Kyoto Protocol with commitments to end energy subsidies and hasten the introduction of renewable energy; (3) recognizing the right to safe drinking water as a basic human right backed by the needed investments; (4) breathing additional life into the biodiversity and desertification conventions and launching an effort to frame country-specific (North–South) compacts to stem deforestation and protect threatened ecosystems and biodiversity hotspots; and (5) revamping global environmental governance and providing new institutional means to set norms and rules of the road for globalization.

In May 2002, the secretary-general issued a major statement based on the "need for greater clarity on what Johannesburg is about and what it can achieve." He called for a "strong program of action" and identified specific areas where "concrete results are both essential and achievable": meeting the clean water and sanitation needs of the poor, providing access to modern energy services to the 2 billion people who now lack them, increasing the use of renewables and energy efficiency, reversing the deterioration of agricultural lands and implementing the Desertification Convention, protecting biodiversity and marine fisheries, and protecting human health from toxic chemicals and unsanitary conditions. These became the five WEHAB areas (water, energy, health, agriculture, and biodiversity), and the U.N. Secretariat produced useful reports in each area. These reports were released shortly before the summit began.

The outcomes of WSSD bore no resemblance to the specific, monitorable plans of action many of us were advocating during the summit's preparatory process. What emerged instead was either nothing, or next to nothing (as in the cases, for example, of renewable energy, desertification, development assistance funding, governance, and globalization), or very general and nonbinding targets with timetables for their accomplishment. The United States and many others typically opposed these targets and timetables, so it was considered a major accomplishment at WSSD when anything vaguely resembling a target and timetable was agreed upon. Among the more notable of these agreements were the following:

- "we agree to halve by the year 2015 . . . the proportion of people who do not have access to basic sanitation";
- we aim to achieve "by 2020 that chemicals are used and produced in ways that lead to the minimization of significant adverse effects on human health or the environment";
- "the following actions are required at all levels: (a) maintain or restore stocks [of fish] to levels that can produce the maximum sustainable yield with the aim of achieving these goals for depleted stocks on an urgent basis and where possible, not later than 2015"; and
- "the achievement by 2010 of a significant reduction in the current rate of loss of biological diversity will require the provision of new and additional financial and technical resources to developing countries."

Clearly, transforming these and the few other time-bound "commitments" in the WSSD Plan of Implementation into major initiatives in the real world will require huge future efforts to move from these generalities to specific plans of action and to garner the necessary political and financial commitments. If this happens, we can look back at the battles at Johannesburg and see these provisions as the start of something important. It is also possible that these agreements will be ignored just as most of the agreements at Rio were. Unfortunately, the Plan of Implementation was silent on follow-up mechanisms for these agreements. As also happened at Rio ten years earlier, the difficult issue of assuring accountability in the implementation process was largely ignored.

There were many other signs of how difficult it was for governments to move the agenda forward at Johannesburg. It was viewed as a signal accomplishment to get the following sentence regarding climate change into the Plan of Implementation: "States that have ratified the Kyoto Protocol strongly urge States that have not already done so to ratify the Kyoto Protocol in a timely manner." That was the summit's only fresh contribution to the most threatening of all environmental problems. Expanded reliance on fossil fuels was called for in numerous places without acknowledgment of climate risks.

Also, negotiators struggled to achieve recognition of the Precautionary Principle previously adopted at Rio. Only a last-minute appeal by Ethiopia managed to delete words that would have made environmental treaties subservient to World Trade Organization rules. The governments also could not agree on language that would guide the WTO on implementing the Doha Agreement or on how to make economic globalization work for sustainable development rather than against it. In the end, many were musing that the day of the U.N. megaconference may have passed.

A more positive assessment of the Johannesburg outcomes is possible if one starts with low expectations and the premise that WSSD was sailing against stiff winds from the outset. In the year before the summit, the world economy had fared poorly. The U.S. administration was preoccupied with the war on terrorism and was generally hostile to both environmental causes and multilateral agreements. The developing world was both wary of and frustrated with the rich countries. The failure to implement the Rio agreements had cast a long shadow, raising questions about credibility and accountability in processes such as WSSD. Those who sought important outcomes at Johannesburg were aware of these and other negative factors, but hoped that the fundamental importance of the issues involved would drive the agenda.

From this perspective many were relieved that what they saw as a generally sensible, forward-looking document was created in the end. They were thankful for modest accomplishments. The targets and timetables on which there was agreement offered some hope. A number of parallel multilateral processes, including several environmental treaties and trade agreements, received a modest boost in the Plan of Implementation, as did the Millennium Development Goals, set at the Millennium Assembly of the United Nations. Poverty and environment linkages received much needed visibility. And the business community was deeply and generally positively involved, much more so than at Rio. Indeed, the developing countries (and development assistance organizations) and the business community left Johannesburg far happier than did the environmental community.

It is important to note that there was tremendous vitality, commitment, and determination within the community of nongovernmental organizations (NGOs) and, indeed, within many of the participating governments and agencies. As a lowest-common-denominator document, however, the WSSD Plan of Implementation was hardly reflective of the best of our world.

WSSD pioneered the promotion of "type-2 outcomes," public-private and other partnership initiatives for sustainable development. Hundreds of these individual initiatives were showcased at Johannesburg. The United States highlighted numerous U.S.-based partnership initiatives, said to be worth $2.4 billion over several years. (Because it offered so little else in the "type-1" negotiations among governments, critics accused the United States of seeking to derail the main purpose of the meeting with type-2 agreements.) The U.N. Environment Programme presented awards for the ten best partnerships, including ones involving Alcan, Inc., for school-based recycling in Asia and the Americas and Shell for a gas exploration project in the Philippines. The United States committed $36 million over three years to help protect Congo Basin forests.

Brazil, the Global Environment Facility (GEF), the World Bank, and the World Wildlife Fund announced one especially promising partnership. Their Amazon Regional Protected Area project ensures that 500,000 square miles of the Amazon will be put under federal protection. This is the largest-ever tropical forest protection plan, covering an area twice the size of the United Kingdom; it will triple the amount of land in the Amazon that is already protected.

In another partnership of a very different sort, Greenpeace and the World Business Council for Sustainable Development joined forces for the first time to call upon governments to tackle climate change on the basis of the Framework Convention on Climate Change and its Kyoto Protocol. Independently, Russia took the occasion of the summit to announce that it would ratify the Kyoto Protocol.

Several other important initiatives announced at Johannesburg planted seeds for the future. The European Union announced that having failed to win green energy targets at WSSD, it would seek to organize a "coalition of the willing," like-minded countries to push ahead with global goals for renewable energy development. Germany's Chancellor Schroeder announced that Germany was willing to host an international conference on renewables, saying that "climate change is no longer a skeptical prognosis but a bitter reality." Another group of like-minded countries, the fifteen biologically richest or "megadiverse" countries that are home to 70 percent of the planet's biological diversity, came together to achieve reductions in the rate of biodiversity loss, protect against biopiracy, and seek fairness and equity in sharing the economic benefits derived from biodiversity.

In sum, one can hope that the sometimes-perverse logic of these affairs might once again come into play. Rio was a great summit with extraordinary momentum during the preparatory process, but the wind went out of its sails shortly after the event. The Johannesburg preparations never developed any forward momentum, but perhaps the frustration and disappointment evident there will spur serious efforts after the event. The postsummit European initiative on renewable energy is an example of what is possible. The WEHAB documents generated late in the process in response to Secretary-General Annan's request provided another important entry point for postsummit action.

What Johannesburg Tells Us

Writing immediately after the Johannesburg Summit, I cannot forecast its long-term significance. But some conclusions are possible.

First, the WSSD was a true sustainable development summit in the sense that advocates of all three dimensions of sustainable development—the "triple bottom line" of economy, environment, and society—were there under one roof arguing their cases, raising real issues, and confronting those with different interests and perspectives. It was not a social summit dealing only with poverty, social exclusion, and human rights. It was not an economic and globalization summit addressing only trade and investment, finance for development, and transfer of technology. And it was not an environmental summit focusing only on large-scale biotic impoverishment and pollution. Johannesburg was instead a summit about the intersections of these issues, and it was as sprawling and unwieldy as the sustainable development concept itself. But, because of this, it accurately reflected the dynamics of these issues as they are in reality today. And every so often, the vision of sustainable development actually becoming the unifying concept for its three powerful components would appear like a quantum apparition, shimmer for a moment, but fade away. Perhaps with more leadership, better preparation, and a more focused agenda, sustainable development fora could provide the meeting ground to resolve real-world issues of inevitable difficulty and complexity. It is doubtful, however, if history is any judge, that the U.N. Commission on Sustainable Development is capable of providing such fora.

As it was, what Johannesburg did reveal in bringing all this together was that our world is badly divided on key issues: corporate accountability, globalization and the WTO, trade and subsidies, climate and energy, development priorities and aid, and many others. The summit debates covered the core issue of making economic globalization supportive of sustainable development, raising many of the right concerns, but in the end delegates could agree only on platitudes and on-the-one-hand, on-the-other-hand. That is a sad but true commentary on the state of international discourse. The warring paradigms discussed in Chapter 1 were much in evidence, and next to nothing was accomplished to bridge this gap in perception and power. In all these senses we are still worlds apart.

Johannesburg also underscored the poor condition we are in regarding the status of environmental issues and institutions. Shortly after the summit, *The Economist* editorialized that "if the world had needed saving, it would have been wrong to expect an event such as the UN summit to rise to that challenge in the first place. Happily, though the world does not need saving. . . . [I]t is ludicrous to suggest that the earth is in grave peril." A sense of mounting alarm regarding the state of the global environment was sometimes hard to find at Johannesburg outside NGO circles and some governments. Seriously wrongheaded though they are, *The Economist's* views did seem to capture a Panglossian perspective that was often present at Johannesburg. The summit revealed that in 2002 the world's governments were more prepared to discuss the economic and social pillars of sustainable development than the environmental pillar. In a similar vein, important questions about how to strengthen multilateral environmental institutions and global environmental governance were never on the table for discussion. The weakness of the summit's Plan of Implementation on environmental issues mirrors the current state of environmental institutions at the international level. The environmental community in and out of government has got its work cut out for it if it is to provide a powerful pillar of sustainable development.

Looking ahead, one area of common endeavor should be concerted efforts to breathe as much life as possible into the agreements reached and initiatives launched at Johannesburg and those that will follow. Also, a transition must take place within institutions and governance. The World Business Council for Sustainable Development (WBCSD), a leading international group of major corporations, has sketched three broad scenarios exploring different paths in environmental governance. One of these paths, called "First Raise Our Growth," or FROG, resolves to solve economic challenges before environmental challenges. FROG is a business-as-usual scenario leading to huge environmental costs. It is a path to failure, even in the eyes of the WBCSD.

In the WBCSD's other two scenarios, sustainability is successfully pursued, but the approaches are very different. Under "GEOPolity," people turn to government to focus the market on environmental and social ends, and they rely heavily on intergovernmental institutions and treaties. Under the "JAZZ" scenario, the world is full of unscripted initiatives that are decentralized and improvisational, like the type-2 initiatives pioneered at Johannesburg. JAZZ provides abundant information about business behavior, and good conduct is enforced by public opinion and consumer decisions. Governments facilitate more than they regulate, NGOs are very active, and businesses see strategic advantages in doing the right thing.

The initial international response to the global-change agenda has been to try to move the world from FROG to GEOPolity. As discussed in Chapter 1, this shift is not yet working very well. Getting serious about the governance transition requires new action on two mutually supportive fronts: pursuing a radically revised approach to GEOPolity, and broadening JAZZ and taking it to scale.

Today's GEOPolity approach is designed to fail. It can be redesigned for success by insisting on new procedures for setting international requirements and on new institutions, including a World Environment Organization (WEO) or the Global Environmental Mechanism (GEM) proposed by Dan Esty and Maria Ivanova in Chapter 5. The case for an effective WEO is as strong as it was for an effective World Trade Organization. The international community knows how to create plausible multilateral arrangements and has done so in other, mostly economic, areas.

There are many innovative ways that the decision-making process in GEOPolity could be improved:

- As has happened with the Montreal Protocol, the Conference of the Parties (COP) to a convention could be empowered to make certain types of regulatory decisions that would not need to be ratified as separate treaties.

- Procedures could be introduced whereby a supermajority, a double majority, or even a mere majority of the COP members could make decisions binding for all.
- The COP could delegate certain rule-making or standard-setting powers to an expert body. The COP would limit itself to providing the broad policy framework and providing a check against abuse of discretion, much as Congress and the federal courts supervise decision making in U.S. regulatory agencies.

Under all of these arrangements, enforcement procedures could be introduced whereby the COP, the treaty secretariat, or an aggrieved party could take a government before a court or some adjudicatory body to compel action. The European Community/European Union has seen a progression in which environmental policy has moved from being the separate province of each European country to being more uniform throughout Europe. The extent of the change is reflected in a recent article in the *New York Times*:

> The European Commission plans to take eight countries to the European Court for not implementing water standards. Britain, Belgium, Spain and Luxembourg failed to meet the December 2000 deadline for drinking water; France, Greece, Germany and Ireland failed to meet standards for waste water or bathing water.

A second path to better governance is to implement measures that can take JAZZ to scale. JAZZ is the most exciting arena for action today, with an outpouring of bottom-up, voluntary initiatives from business, governments, NGOs, and others, such as the following:

- Seven large companies—DuPont, Shell, BP Amoco, and Alcan among them—have agreed to reduce their greenhouse gas emissions 15 percent below their 1990 levels by 2010. Alcoa is reported to be on track to reduce its emissions to 25 percent below 1990 levels in this time frame, and DuPont is on schedule to reduce emissions by 65 percent by 2010.
- Eleven major companies—including DuPont, General Motors, and IBM—have formed the Green Power Market Development Group and committed to developing markets for 1,000 megawatts of renewable energy over the next decade.
- Home Depot, Lowe's, Andersen, and others have agreed to sell wood (to the degree that it is available) that is harvested only from sustainably

managed forests certified by an independent group against rigorous criteria. Unilever, the largest processor of fish in the world, has agreed to do the same regarding fish products.

NGOs have played important roles in forging these corporate initiatives. They are the real maestros of JAZZ. State and local governments, private foundations, universities, and other entities also have contributed. Through the International Council for Local Environmental Initiatives, more than five hundred local governments are now part of a campaign to reduce greenhouse gas emissions. The Pew Center on Global Climate has identified twenty-one separate state initiatives to reduce greenhouse gas emissions.

There is much that can be done to encourage and support JAZZ. Possibilities range all the way from simple public recognition to encouragement through means such as WSSD's type-2 initiatives, to governmental actions such as mandated disclosures of environmental impacts and costs, and creative use of governmental purchasing power.

The transition to good governance for environment and sustainable development will also require a dramatic strengthening in at least three other areas. First is the need to rapidly build capacities for capable, transparent, and democratic governments. Major new resources should be made available for building technical, management, and leadership capacities in developing societies. Second, both creativity and resources should be brought to the forging of "compacts" or "bargains" between the rich countries of the North and poorer countries of the South. Under these arrangements, poorer countries take impressive steps to halt deforestation and biodiversity loss, for example, and rich countries provide financial and other support for these efforts and for the poorer countries' economic priorities. And third, using modern criteria for organizational design, it should be possible to create new and innovative arrangements associated with the United Nations to address these central goals.

References

Annan, K. 2002. "Towards a Sustainable Future," address at the American Museum of Natural History, May 14, 2002.

Anon. 2002. "EU Seeks Green Energy Goals after Summit Defeat," *World Environmental News* (www.planetark.org), June 9, 2002.

Anon. 2002. "Small Is Alright," *The Economist,* September 7, 2002, page 13.

Anon. 2002. "Water Standards Not Met," *New York Times,* February 23, 2002, page A7.

Czuczka, T. 2002. "Germany Pushes for Renewable Energy Conference," *Environmental News Network,* (www.enn.com), September 6, 2002.

Pomeroy, R. 2002. "Industry Joins Greenpeace to Demand Climate Action," *World Environment News,* (www.planetark.org), August 30, 2002.

Strong, M. 2001. Remarks at the United Nations University Conference on the World Summit on Sustainable Development, September 3, 2001.

United Nations World Summit on Sustainable Development. 2002. *Plan of Implementation* (advanced unedited text, September 4, 2002).

World Business Council for Sustainable Development. 1997. *Exploring Sustainable Development: Global Scenarios 2000–2050.* Geneva: WBCSD.

World Wildlife Fund. 2002. "WSSD on Energy: Nothing for the Poor, Nothing for the Climate," September 3, 2002 (WWF Global Network [www.panda.org]).

Index